Ends of the World

CECILY MACKWORTH

ENDS of the WORLD

CARCANET

First published in Great Britain in 1987 by
Carcanet Press Limited
208-212 Corn Exchange Buildings,
Manchester M4 3BQ

Carcanet
198 Sixth Avenue
New York
New York 10013

The publisher acknowledges financial assistance
from the Arts Council of Great Britain

British Library Cataloguing in Publication Data

Mackworth, Cecily
  Ends of the world.
  1. Mackworth, Cecily   2. Journalists—
  Great Britain—Biography
  I. Title
  070'.92'4   PN5123.M3/

ISBN 0-85635-638-7

Typeset in 11/12½ pt Garamond by Koinonia Limited, Manchester
Printed in England by SRP Ltd, Exeter

Preface

In the different chapters of this book, I have tried to trace the various stages of a journey through a changing world. It is about cities or countries which I left knowing that something had come to an end there, and that something else was beginning. Change is its real subject. Details about my private life could only be irrelevant. They belong to another book, which it is unlikely I shall ever write. In the same way, if I were now to do research, look up exact dates, check personal experience against newspaper reports, this book might be more useful to historians but it would not recreate events as they exist in memory, or as I reconstitute them from scraps of diaries or jotted notes. During this period which covers, roughly, the years 1937 to 1960, I was a spectator, roaming in a no-man's-land between past and future. I write from the viewpoint of this spectator and from no other. The title *Ends of the World* sums up, in fact, exactly what the book is about.

Cecily Mackworth

I

One has to begin somewhere. There is a choice to be made: this moment or that, memory laid out like a map, with a flag-pin to mark: it began here, or there. Yet, looking back, I can see that every beginning has also been an end – the end of childhood, the end of adolescence, the end of the world as I knew it in early youth. . . The day, for instance, when I stood with Jeanne Bucher on the balcony of her art gallery in the boulevard Montparnasse and heard the distant thudding of guns in the eastern suburbs. Her stern old face had turned quite white aid she said in a low clear voice, speaking straight out into the air, 'Now God is dead.'

That seems to me as good an end, or as good a beginning, as any that can be dredged up from the past. The world was toppling into chaos, as it has done so many times in the course of history, and then rearranged itself laboriously into some kind of order. This time, though, I was watching it happening, conscious, though still in a somewhat confused way, that a familiar country lay at my back and a new, still uncharted one was opening up in front of me.

It was not mere chance that had dropped me at that precise moment on that balcony in Montparnasse. Something had brought me to Paris first, though what it was is difficult to determine without going further and further back. Wanting to discover Love and Art, wanting to escape. . . finding instead loneliness. Those cheap *pensions de famille*; those grim-faced assistants at the Sorbonne, asking for certificates I did not possess; a Montparnasse full of worried Jews escaped from Hitler's Germany, nothing like the romantic Bohemia of so many memoirs.

Dazed by the beauty of Paris, I wandered alone by the banks of the Seine, watching Flemish barges gliding in from the north, and patient fishermen angling for sprats. I sat in Notre-Dame, eyes fixed on the cardinals' hats dangling above the high altar. When one of them dropped, someone had told me, the cardinal's soul would be freed from purgatory but this never happened in my presence. I went to the Surrealist Exhibition and saw artificial rain droppng on a crocodile seated in the back of a battered old motor-car. I went several times to Sylvia Beach's bookshop, Shakespeare & Co., near the carrefour de l'Odéon and once to Adrienne Monnier's French bookshop just opposite. Maybe I saw famous writers there. Maybe Ernest Hemingway was there, ruffling through the pages of his own works, or James Joyce, sulking in a corner. If I did see them I didn't recognize them. I met a few artists too – elegant little Viera da Silva, whose canvases were all tiny blobs of colour, brilliant as jewels; her husband, Arpad Szenes, who told me stories of a brief moment in the history of Hungary when artists had been the true kings of his country; William Hayter, whose engravings were so icily perfect that it seemed there was nothing to be said about them: people, places, happenings, all seemed to be part of a country through whose guarded frontiers I peered with little hope of ever crossing them.

One afternoon – it was late in the summer of 1937 – I drifted into a picture gallery in Montparnasse, simply because I had nowhere special to go. A young man strolled in the empty room – eyes the colour of wintry water and an appearance so insignificant that he might have served as a model for one of those Le Carré spies who did not yet exist. We talked; he said he was a painter; I told him I wanted to write. He gave me an icy stare and said, 'You must meet Henry Miller.'*

He led me at a brisk pace down the boulevard Raspail, round by the great bronze Lion of Belfort, and into the rue de la

---

* Henry Miller (1891-1980), novelist. *Tropic of Cancer* (1934) and *Tropic of Capricorn* (1938) were published in Paris but banned for many years in the USA and Britain. Perlès wrote a study of his work, *My Friend Henry Miller* (London, 1955).

Tombe Issoire in the fourteenth arrondissement, which was then a long, dingy street, full of shops selling ironmongery, artificial silk underwear and cheap stationery. The Villa Seurat opened off it – a cul-de-sac, blocked by trees at one end and bordered with low houses and tiny gardens with flowering shrubs sprouting through iron railings. It was like the décor for a Balzac novel, but in fact it was inhabited almost entirely by various kinds of artists and intellectuals. Approaching, we could hear subdued sounds of their activities – tapping of a sculptor's hammer, bursts of Mozart, clatter of typewriters. 'Ubac and Soutine live here,' said my guide, quite casually.*

Henry Miller lived in a studio at number 18. Someone opened the door and I stepped into the world of the Villa Seurat.

There were a lot of people standing about or sitting on the floor. A corkscrew staircase led up to a loggia. A gramophone was playing 'Stormy Weather'. Henry himself was rather bald, spectacled, already middle-aged. . . a general impression of untidiness. . . clothes rumpled, perhaps not very clean. . . an eager, concentrated look, as if he was waiting for something to happen and wanted to be ready for it. Later, I realized he was waiting for the moment when he would want to write.

When the writing moment came, it made no special difference. If there were visitors, they went on playing jazz on the gramophone, reading their poetry aloud to each other or doing whatever they happened to be doing at the time. Henry just moved over to the table in the corner and started to write. Once he began, he went on, apparently never feeling the need to take a walk or go to bed. He wrote on without fuss; pages of *Tropic of Capricorn* piled up beside him while the red wine in the bottle at his elbow sank lower and lower. After a time, someone – generally Alfred Perlès – would bring him a plate of food, to be forked messily into his mouth with one hand, while he went on typing with the other. Twenty-four hours

* Raoul Ubac (b. 1910), painter; Chaim Soutine (1893-1943), one of the foremost Expressionists.

at a stretch were nothing to him. He would go on until he had said whatever he wanted to say. Then, suddenly, it was time to stop, time to do something different, time to disappear into that still-censored world I discovered years later when, returning to Paris, I found French translations of the two *Tropics* on open sale in the bookshops.

This remarkable resistance to fatigue must have been partly due to physical stamina, somewhat fortified by drink. I think, though, that it was above all the result of an intellectual attitude which refused to admit barriers or limitations to human existence. Henry believed that people could do whatever they want to do, and that the trouble with most of them was that they did not want enough. If you wanted to write, you sat down and wrote; if you wanted to write poetry, you sat down and wrote poetry. Grammar, vocabulary and so on were just accessories. 'A real poet can write poetry in any language,' he said, and showed me as proof a poem for his friend Hans Reichel, written in German, a language of which he had only the scantiest knowledge.

Later experience has taught me that writers in general are greatly afraid of wasting either their time or their ideas. I don't think such parsimony ever occurred to Henry. He participated energetically in whatever was going on, such as frying beefsteaks on the gas burner, cranking up the gramophone, or making sudden dashes out to the local cinema, or playing Russian billiards in the café on the place d' Alésia. Henry liked this café because it was a working-class sort of place which gave him a rest from intellectuals. Just one year earlier the workers had gained the right to holidays with pay, and the excitement of these holidays was still fresh. There were generally groups of men – wives did not go much to cafés in those days – drinking white wine or *calva* at the counter and exchanging stories of their first glimpse of the sea or of bicycle trips along the Loire. Like me, they too were discovering new regions of experience.

Henry had a number of close friends, each of whom played a separate but essential part in his life. Quite a lot of them were

Henry Miller, Louveciennes c. 1933

Lawrence Durrell, Paris 1937

younger than he was, so that one sometimes had the impression of a benevolent uncle, or perhaps one of those gurus who refuse to take themselves seriously and dispense wisdom in jokey, throw-away phrases. Some of these friends became woven for a time into my own life. Lawrence Durrell, just arrived from Corfu, had brought with him the manuscript of *The Black Book*. He was about twenty-five then – short and sturdy and radiating a kind of force which made it seem that his whole body was charged with static electricity. A great worker, constantly creating, always on the alert, absorbing everything he saw and heard, recreating it, mingling it with his own thoughts, perceptions, ideas. Although he worked so much, and drank more than was good for him, he was tremendously generous with his time, wanting to know exactly what everyone was doing, bursting with praise if he liked it and making forthright criticisms if he did not. He and Henry had been corresponding for nearly two years and were throbbing with excitement about each other's work. The meeting might have been catastrophic, but as it turned out, they seemed to complete each other in some way – Henry more of a moralist, Larry more of a poet. They exchanged abrasive criticism and delirious praise, and each seemed to heighten the tension of the other's creative life.

Alfred Perlès (Fredl) – an old crony and Henry's accomplice in literary and other adventures – was living in the Villa Seurat at the time. Small, thin and dark, as I remember him, with shiny brown eyes which always looked a little frightened, though what he was afraid of nobody knew, including, I think, himself. Pursued by this undefined panic, he drank, made friends in strange places, chased women, took whatever jobs would ensure him a minimal existence. His parents were prosperous Viennese Jews, so they must have heard a good deal about Freud, and surely disapproved of him. This may have accounted for Fredl's obsession with the subconscious – a region less open to the public than it is today. When I first came to the Villa Seurat, he was editing a magazine handed down to him, for some unexplained reason, by the American Country Club. Fredl had an immediate vision of an influential literary magazine. Henry and Larry had been co-opted on to the editorial board and Larry dashed to London in search of contributors, undaunted by the fame of T. S. Eliot and George Orwell. Only three numbers appeared, leaving the original subscribers sadly puzzled by this sudden change of style. The fourth and last was entitled 'Air-conditioned Womb Number', and consisted of variations on the then little-known Freudian back-to-the-womb theory, with speculations as to what might be encountered along that seductive but dangerous passage. One of the articles was by Anaïs Nin.* I met her only once, briefly. She was lying on a sofa, looking like a lithe, beautiful

---

* Anaïs Nin (1903-1977), writer. She is known chiefly for her journals, which she kept continuously from the age of eleven. Many volumes have been published in Britain, the USA and most European countries.

9

cat.

The Womb Number was soft suicide. Letters poured in with heavily underscored accusations of obscenity and demands for return of subscriptions. The editors washed their hands of the whole affair; the magazine had been fun, but had been beguiling them from serious work.

Then there was David Edgar, who had first introduced me to the Villa Seurat. He was a somewhat clandestine painter whose work was seldom if ever seen, and who spoke either not at all or in a compulsive, hypnotic torrent about his inner torments. And there was Hans Reichel, the German painter, who lived in the same house and was admired and envied by Henry and Larry because neither of them could be content to express himself only in writing. They too painted by fits and starts and were saddened because they could not produce paintings as beautiful as his. It is not Reichel himself that I remember, but the lovely abstract water-colours he brought to the studio and propped round the walls for us to admire. There was Conrad Moricand, the astrologer – a dark, creepy man who made me feel uneasy. I never dared to ask him what the stars had in store for me. And other, shadowy figures who have faded, like so much else, from my memory.

I wonder if other things have faded too? Is it possible that we were so absorbed in the excitement of just living that we did not feel the shadows closing in on us? Didn't we realize that our world was about to fall apart? There must surely have been doubts and premonitions, but in my presence at least no one mentioned them. I think that Henry, who was the oldest and the leader, wanted to enjoy a doomed world before it crumbled away. He wanted to write and paint and talk and explore the byways of the mind while this could still be done. There were only a few months to go before the Villa Seurat would stand empty, deserted by its inhabitants. The street lights would be put out and Paris would become a cold, quiet city that waited and waited for something to happen.

Then it did happen, and Jeanne Bucher leaned from her balcony and said, 'Now God is dead.'

II

Scientists tell me that in pure theory, it could be possible to discover some way of travelling faster than light. If this should ever happen, our present notion of time would become obsolete, and we should be forced to admit a fact we all recognize in our hearts but prefer in general to ignore: that we live simultaneously in two dimensions. In one, facts and figures are important, clocks and calendars exist to keep us on the rails. In the other, we are carried along on unknown tides, perhaps the same which bear us from point to point in our dreams. There, time is no longer something which can be measured; it exists only according to the way we experience it. Precipitated into its current at times of extreme tension, born away by violence or delight, we can only surrender to it until, cast back at last on familiar shores, we wonder: how long did it really last?

So there is no measure for the time between the moment we heard the thudding of German guns on the outskirts of Paris, and that other moment when I found myself on the road that cuts straight across the wide plain of the Beauce. Here I am, consciousness active once more, just long enough to register the landscape, my nearest companions, and myself. On either side fields of ripening corn melt into the blue heat-haze on the horizon. Straight ahead rise the twin towers of Chartres, etched sharp against the sky. Refugees beside me, behind me, before me. From above, we must look like a column of drugged ants. We trudge, shedding belongings by the roadside. Goodbye to the bronze statuette of Geography, pride of some family mantelpiece; goodbye to the battered motor-car, of no use to anyone since there will not be any more petrol; goodbye even to the last wheelbarrow, loaded high with tins of food and mattresses with tufts of wool sticking out of their ticking.

11

When the planes sweep out of the sky, graceful as seagulls, to spray us with shrapnel, there is just time to throw ourselves into the ditch. Piled one on top of the other, we cease to be our own, individual selves, become just an amalgam of bodies, breath held too tight to scream. . . but afterwards patches of blood shine bright on parched brown grass. Someone calls 'Nurse! Nurse!' because I am still wearing the uniform the Red Cross gave me when I was helping at Austerlitz station with the refugees from Belgium and the north, who were flooding into Paris as the Germans advanced. I am helpless and ignorant, a cheat in this disguise. If there was only a bandage, or just a clean handkerchief, I might try tying up a wound, but there is nothing. Once I poured eau-de-cologne into a red, smelly hole. It made me feel useful.

On we trudge. A dog sidles through various pairs of legs, picks on me for possible adoption. A child runs screaming and searching. Old people sit down by the wayside and give up the effort. Soldiers have turned us away from the road to Chartres, heading us off into some other direction. A sudden vision of that perfect rose-window. . . just time to wonder if it is lying in a heap of shattered glass on the floor.

We grew hungrier and dirtier. There were fewer and fewer of us. People were being suctioned off by rest-centres, charitable committees, provincial relations. I moved onward, not knowing whether I was going south, east or west. Farmers gave lifts in their carts; soldiers hoisted me on to army vehicles. I was fed on strawberries – a record crop that year and about all that was left to eat since the first waves of refugees had passed. Once or twice, someone took me home to sleep in a real bed and to eat strawberries with a fork or spoon. It was in Nantes, I think – but perhaps further south – that we heard Marshal Pétain's quavery old voice, relayed by radio from a scratchy recording, 'It is with a broken heart that I tell you we must cease the fight. . .'.

Next day I heard it again from the radio set in a bistro where they served ground acorns in the guise of coffee. A lot of people had crowded in to hear the broadcast. A woman began

Refugees leaving Paris, 1940

to cry, wailing in an artificial way as if she thought it was expected of her. But a man laughed, banging his glass on the counter: 'That's done with the war! To hell with the lot of them!' A soldier, drunk already, staggered to the door and tossed his rifle into the bushes: 'No more use for that! It would never have gone off anyway. It was all rusted up when they gave it to me.'

So it must, it ought to be, back to England, and quickly. I thought of Bordeaux, where there might be a ship, if I could ever get there; of the Pyrenees, which I might cross if ever I could reach them. Yet I made no real effort, took no advantage of possible opportunities. I went wherever chance took me and now, much later, it seems to me that I had a vague feeling of belonging to that particular time and place. History was building up all around me and I felt involved, part of it, wanting to wait a little longer and see it taking shape.

I moved southward only slowly, frightened yet exhilarated.

13

There were towns and villages, places passed through, lingered in, left. Painted signs at the entry to some village signalled a name, but memory has often displaced these names, setting some place in a valley where it should have been on a hill, endowing another with a fine Norman church which was never there. Certain events cannot have happened in the region where I remember them: soup given here, biscuits refused there; a confusion of splintered recollections, rather like groping in a half-remembered dream when logical connections have dissolved in daylight, or perhaps never existed.

I came to Aubusson, in the mountainous centre of France. With no recollection of the roads which led me to it or the transport which brought me there, the little town reappears in memory isolated, as if floating in space. The main square, it seems to me, was close to the river, with the old town rising behind it. Something about that square in which I so inexplicably found myself, suggested peace, industry, decency. Those solid houses evoked a prosperous bourgeoisie, occupied for centuries in producing glowing tapestries for lords and princes of their day. It was not a proper setting for the cross, ragged crowd which had taken possession of the café terraces or roamed aimlessly, enquiring from each other about shelter for the night or when the railway station was going to open.

I thought of Jean Lurçat, the great modern tapestry-maker, whom I had met once, when Jeanne Bucher exhibited his work in her gallery. He was a native of this town. I wondered if I might perhaps meet him and if he would recognize me.

Then, almost at once, I recognized his bald head, looked again and it was indeed him, crossing the *place* with the assured step of a man in his home-town, contrasting curiously with the harassed expression of refugees who knew themselves to be universally unwelcome. This face, revealing itself so unexpectedly among the surrounding mass of anonymous, greyish features, appeared like a sign of some sort of order emerging out of chaos.

Jean Lurçat took me to a tall old house overlooking the

14

river. The living-room walls were covered with designs ready for tracing on to canvas backings. He and his Polish wife had left all their belongings in Paris, or had perhaps lost them on the way, and they were living penniless now on the charity of friends. They fed me with what they had – a little milk and those beans which were the staple diet now the strawberry crop was over. They lent me their son's bed for the night. He had left them a day earlier, taking a macintosh and a tin of corned beef. His mother could not speak of him. When she tried to, her breath caught in her throat and she could only say, 'I am afraid. . . afraid. . .'.

He arrived the next day. Seventeen, corn-yellow hair, turquoise-blue eyes and that ephemeral beauty which exists only in very young men, when they are hovering between boyhood and early manhood, and which makes one fear for what will happen to them. He told us he had been with friends, preparing hide-outs in the woods. One of the masters from his college had secret contacts and had warned them the Germans were planning to conscript young men for work in Germany. He was glowing with happiness, wanting to reassure his parents, yet enjoying at the same time this clandestine life he was about to enter and had promised to keep from them.*

After that, other people begin to take clearer form in my memory. No longer shadowy figures emerging for a moment out of the flow of time, but real individuals with distinct faces, voices, homes of their own: Jean and Katia Lurçat; Marie-Marguerite, captain of the local girl-guide troop; Monsieur Bourgeois, who taught mathematics at the college; Monsieur and Madame Sallandrouse, so grave and respectable, conscious that their family had ruled the town for a couple of centuries; the thin, gentle chemist whose name I have forgotten. . .

Here they are, gathered in the dispensary, which is really the school library. Here I spend my days and nights. Under the table, the mattress on which I sleep. Floor piled with

---

* Victor Lurçat was later able to escape through Spain to the United States. He enlisted in the American Army and was killed during the Normandy landings. – C.M.

textbooks; shelves cleared for bottles from the chemist's meagre stock – disinfectant, cough medicine, ear-drops, eye-drops, a few syringes.

Patients arrive before I have time to heat my ersatz coffee on the spirit-burner. A soldier with a nasty head-wound, another with a bullet in his shoulder, a woman whose child has a running ear and screams before I touch him. How did they get here? They tell long, confused stories of skirmishes in the north or weeks of tramping along hot, aimless roads. I remember a sign at the entry to the town, pointing to the hospital. Why don't they go to it? Marie-Marguerite explains in her precise, convent-bred voice, 'Well, you see, there aren't any doctors or nurses left. Just Dr Lantier, but he's nearly ninety, you know, and he felt he really wasn't up to it.'

A soldier bares his thigh, holds out a penknife. 'Go on, I trust you.' It isn't me he trusts. It's a ragged overall with a red cross stitched over the breast. I pour disinfectant, scoop gingerly. 'You going to pass out, Nurse? Give it to me, I'll have a go myself.' The head of the bullet appears. Not very deep. I seize it with my pincers, pull. It comes out nicely and I lay it in a saucer. Delivering a baby must be something like this.

Some time in the afternoon a boy-scout arrives, panting, to say that a lorry full of English soldiers is parked in the square and no one can understand them. One of them had blood on his head and they were pointing at him to show he needed help.

Some soldiers and a small, very young officer stood beside an ordinary French military van, with a few more inside, sleeping with their heads on each other's shoulders. They were so dirty, ragged and unshaven that they had quite lost any national trait. They might have been French or Greek or Polish troops, but one of them said, 'Thank Gawd, here's a Christian at last!' with a comfortable Midlands accent.

There was a lot of crusted blood on the wounded man's head but they could not stop even five minutes more. They must be on their way, to try to reach Marseilles, take ship for Egypt, get there before the Germans closed the port.

I asked them if they had news from England, but they knew

even less then I did. 'Hurry! Hurry!' said the officer as I bandaged the wound. He had a nervous twitch in one eye. 'Come on, Miss,' said one of the soldiers. 'You come along with us and take a look at the pyramids.' Then the lorry creaked away, one of the men holding the wounded boy's head in his lap.

The first newspapers appeared on the streets. Vendors shouted, 'Armistice signed! Read about the terms!'

Next day, a ceremony was held at the foot of the war memorial in the main square. The weather had broken and rain dripped on processions of scouts and girl-guides carrying banners at half-mast. A group of orphans, hurriedly dressed in mourning and shepherded by black-clad nuns, began to cry as they grew wetter and wetter. Such notables as could be found made speeches beneath a hastily-constructed shelter: 'This is for us a day of mourning but also a day of hope. . .' The townspeople wept under their umbrellas but the refugees, used to being unwelcome everywhere, huddled on the outskirts of the crowd, asking each other if they would be able to return now to their homes.

Up in the schoolhouse, Monsieur Bourgeois had been twiddling each evening at his wireless-set. Broadcasts from the BBC had crackled and screeched, emitting only a few intelligible words, but at least one knew England was still there, carrying on somehow, not yet crushed or invaded. Then one evening, it must have been the day after we had mourned or celebrated the Armistice, there was an invitation to dinner from Madame Sallandrouse. Cousins had arrived by bicycle from Tours and brought a few supplies. There was good wine from the family cellar, plush upholstery in the salon; portraits of ancestors in decent, sober costumes, not aping the aristocracy but knowing themselves more competent, more sensible, better behaved. Monsieur Sallandrouse bent over the cumbersome old wireless-set on the Louis-Philippe commode, twiddling its knobs, with his pointed grey beard, stiff collar and dark suit, looking strangely like his own great-grandfather gazing down on him from the wall. In Bordeaux or wherever the government might be, they were droning out the usual exhortations to do our duty, about work, patriotism and how France was going to play her part in a new Europe. The Sallandrouse family and their cousins nodded gravely, reassured by words that had been losing their meaning for too many years. Then another twiddle, and suddenly a new voice, miraculously audible: 'We have lost a battle but not the war. . . I ask all Frenchmen to join me in London. . .'. General de Gaulle brought hope to some, and roused the fury of others, and destroyed the sad yet comfortable resignation which had spread like a blanket over France.

As for myself, I knew instantly that I must return to England. For weeks, I had been floating in space, free and rootless, waiting for some sign which would determine my way, and almost wishing it would never come. I had wanted to be homeless and stateless, to create, step by hesitating step, a future untramelled by the past. And now I was suddenly homesick, impatient to be gone.

Limoges, they told me, was the place to go. There was a City Prefect there, some sort of order had been restored and the famous porcelain manufactory had reopened. The solid bourgeoisie of Aubusson had connections with the still more solid bourgeoisie of Limoges. So one morning I set off in a bus with a band of sleepy workmen, rattling over the hilly roads into the Haute Vienne.

In Limoges there was indeed a City Prefect and I was shown without difficulty into his office in the Town Hall. He was a tall scrawny man with a meagre moustache, and I suspected him of having appointed himself to this post. He seemed to be organizing the city into a crazy sort of order. Refugees – uncontrollable, unhealthy and mostly dirty – were his enemies. I had no right, he told me, to be in his town, but now I was there, I had no right to leave it. Not only would he give me no help to go any further, he would prevent me from doing so. He showed me posters, issued in the name of the French Republic and of Marshal Pétain. Roads, they said were to be used only by authorized persons; boundaries were not to be crossed. Movement of any kind was abhorrent to this man. 'Now you are here,' he said, 'you must remain here.' It was like the game we used to play as children – when the music stopped one had to freeze in whatever position one found oneself. Such restrictions were totally unrelated to real life and I soon found that no one had power to enforce them. I no longer believed in such games, so I rested a day then walked, hitched rides and came to Toulouse, where there was rumoured to be some kind of consul.

Rose-red walls flicker in the sunlight. Shops full of crystalized violets, but long queues waiting by the bakeries. I wait my turn, buy bread, eat it in the deep shadows of a thirteenth-century cathedral, sleep a little in a high, carved-oak pew.

Late afternoon: something has changed, those quiet streets are full of people now. Talking and angry shouting. A boy appears with a bundle of newspapers. The papers snatched away, gone in a moment. People push and jostle. I stand on tiptoe, read over someone's shoulder, 'British attack French fleet at Mers-el-Kebir.'

They are shouting now, 'Murderers! Assassins!', eyes gleaming with hatred, more frightening by far than the German bombs. If these people guess the truth, they will turn on me, beat me, claw at my face, trample on me. A man beside me says in a reasonable voice: 'You can't believe all they tell you in the newspapers.' Someone hits out at him and sends him spinning into a letter-box. People start fighting – they have had a signal – but in a desultory way, as if they want revenge but can't find an adequate enemy. The fight sways backwards and forwards across the street till two policemen run up, blowing their whistles.

The Consul was Belgian, with a drawer full of rubber-stamps left by departed colleagues. A distracted young man, besieged by refugees who had fled to France from somewhere, mad to escape again: Spaniards, escaped over the Pyrenees from the Guardia Civil, herded into camps on the outskirts of this city, broken out now and not a bit of paper between them;

German Jews too, prepared to queue night and day for a visa to anywhere; Poles, Czechs, Hungarians, enlisted in the French Foreign Legion, knowing better than to wait for the Nazis; Frenchmen making for England, Spain, Algiers; French who were there simply because their identity papers had been lost, stolen, destroyed. Without them they panicked, suspecting they themselves had ceased to exist.

My own passport lay buried beneath the rubble of the railway station in Rennes, about a thousand kilometres away. I had found myself there because, somewhere on the journey, I had happened on a train which was supposed to be going to Cherbourg, where there might have been a ship for England. The train had panted and grunted and stopped for hours in remote places where peasants came hurrying over the fields with cans of water, which they sold to us by the mug at high prices. In Rennes, a loudspeaker had announced that the train would go no further. What happened after that? I remember a café and the sharp taste of lemonade, then wailing sirens and someone pushing me down the steps into a shelter. When I returned to daylight, my little case had disappeared and my passport with it. Accustomed to the haphazard English attitude in these matters, I had accepted its loss with a nonchalence which had baffled functionaries all along my route. Now I realized for the first time the importance of documents proving one's name, nationality, date and place of birth. Without them I was no longer myself, nor indeed anyone else. All around people wept and screamed because they were paperless like me, and presently I might be weeping and screaming just as they were. Even the Consul was screaming, waving his arms to drive us all away, gesticulating in vain efforts to drive away our menacing horde.

Miracles do happen. One of them occurred there in Toulouse, in that stuffy, crowded, stinking office. A door leading to some inner sanctum opened and framed in it stood an elderly man with a familiar face. It was a distant relation from Belgium, a sort of cousin who had once been in the consular service. He recognized me, dirty and fatigued as I was, and I left the office with a passport, false in every detail. Even the photo from the photomaton machine only dimly resembled what I had believed to be my face.

Marseilles now. A ship, outlined sharp against the dark blue sky, lay far out to sea, balancing on gentle waves. Nobody knew why it was there or where it was going. People stood along the quays, luggage piled beside them, gazing at it hungrily. The Maritime Bureau was in a state of siege, but employees turned their backs, shouted over their shoulders that it was no business of theirs.

The Vieux Port was full of Spaniards, looking exactly like those in Limoges, wearing the same berets and grimy singlets. They sat under striped umbrellas on the café terraces, sometimes playing cards but mostly just gazing out to sea. A few had hired boats and could be seen rowing away to nowhere.

Spanish Consulate, Portuguese Consulate. . . German Jews compared snippets of information. Visas for a few of them, for most an indifferent refusal, a waving away, no argument possible, only angry shouting in unknown languages and guards in foreign uniforms to drive away the importunate. Shifty-eyed men slipping among them, proposing a passage over the Pyrenees. News relayed back from the frontier post: customs officers will shut their eyes for ten thousand pesetas, not a sou less. In the cafés on the Canébière, coins chink on marble-topped tables, counted and recounted. *Nicht genug. . . Immer nicht genug.* A woman, they say, cut her throat just outside the Portuguese Consulate. No one has bothered to mop up the blood.

In Marseilles, food supplies had been mysteriously plentiful, but in Perpignan one could walk for an hour before finding bread and a piece of garlic-sausage to chew. It was already a Spanish city, with great ramparts hewn from red sandstone and tall, dark houses huddling close to its walls. Its people too were lean and dark. Men sat in rows on benches or low walls, following intruders with resentful eyes, spitting and passing remarks in a rocky Catalan dialect. One could tell when a consulate was somewhere near because of the queue stretching along the street. This was the last-chance town. Afterwards, there would be just little Port-Vendres, not really a town at all, then Spain.

I had my visas and found a place in a military train that sauntered through flat sand-dunes. When it halted, I watched Senegalese troops bathing in patches of salt lake or squatting beside the water, washing their clothes, rubbing them between flat stones. This strange lunar landscape and the glistening black bodies seemed to belong to a no-man's-land, a zone beyond the frontiers of reality. Further on, one might perhaps find oneself in some quite unimaginable country.

I was unsurprised to learn that the frontier was now closed again.

I set out in the early morning and the fierce August heat was already burning down, scorching my back through my thin blouse. The track was steep but not really difficult or dangerous. At first it wound up through abandoned vineyards, then between boulders and low scrub and sometimes tracts of sandy earth covered with thyme and rock-rose. The air smelt of salt, scorched grass and tangy plants. Goats nuzzled the rocks, searching for blades of grass. Sometimes a twist in the path revealed great scars, dried-up river-beds, dropping dizzily down to a dark-green sea with moving patches of purple-black shadow. Sometimes there were glimpses of Port-Vendres and tiny white-washed houses which gradually became just a spatter of whiteness shining in the sun.

When the track began to wind downhill, I guessed I had passed the frontier. A minute guard-post belonged to a new country. At some unmarked point. I had taken my last step in France and my first in Spain. Another end, or another beginning and nothing to mark the divide.

How beautiful is Lisbon, white in the African heat. The fawn-coloured country gashed open by the Tagus like a sapphire wound, and the white town, tier upon tier, with its avenues and palm trees and wedding-cake churches. The women sway like butterflies, flat baskets of shining fish balanced on their little cameo heads and frightful Portuguese curses on their lips. The pink and blue boats bob on the Tagus and their names tell one something about Portugal: 'My little, plump-breasted Teresa under the protection of the Sacred Heart of Jesus.'

How beautiful is Lisbon, into which flow the drains of Europe. The scum, the flotsam and jetsam, the excrement of the world, the humiliated and insulted, the outcasts. They come from every corner of Europe, their faces scarred by the police of a hundred lands, and they stand by the banks of the Tagus and look out over the shinging blue sea, over thousands of miles of flat shining sea, towards a country which has never existed. They would like to roll up their clothes from their seamed and knotted legs and wade out into the pale sea, further and further, farther and farther, until this cruel continent becomes only a memory behind them. Then they count the leagues of the sea and its fathoms and turn away, their oozing feet dragging on the sands and they mount the white tiers of the city, to the street of the Consulates, and there they will stand – for ever, this time – holding out ragged, multicoloured passports which demand so little, only the impossible, one more visa, a little ink and a stamp and the goodwill of mankind.

The Spaniards had been mad as hatters, one-eyed, one-armed, clanking with medals, and conversing in patriotic catch-words. The Portuguese are gentle and melancholy. They often use the word *saudades*, which means nostalgia and melancholy and that everything is better in the imagination than it is in reality. In between attacks of *saudades* they spit purposefully, shout for the pleasure of making a noise and pinch my behind as I climb the hill to the Pensão Valentina. At Portuguese bullfights there is no death and the bull walks out of the arena as friskily as he entered it.

But there is plenty of death in Portugal, polite, gentle death. By now I know so much about death that I recognize it when

23

I see it. There is no violence, it is a saudadish death and those who undergo it come from so much violence that it takes them a long time to understand that they are just ghosts, dragging their chains, headless for all eternity. They stand, positively transparent, upon the shores of the Tagus and gaze out to sea. Sometimes a ship anchors in the harbour and picks up a few of them, and off they go, rolling away in the direction of the Azores, meek under the ironic eyes of the Swedish or American or Japanese sailors. They take their heads with them but they are not so lucky as the Portuguese bulls.

Sometimes I feel that I am a Portuguese, with an overdose of *saudades*; sometimes my nose crooks and thickens and my shoulders thicken and bend and the dark walls of the Polish ghetto close around me. Sometimes I am even Abraham Laquadem, and my body aches from the wanderings of two thousand years, and my eyes ache with watching the history of the world and my ears with its clamour and tumult. And then, since I have been carrying my head under my arm for some months now, I am the *statenlos* woman who cut her throat outside the Portuguese Consulate in Marseilles.

And meanwhile, here I am, chugging across the Tagus in the steamer ferry to eat lobster with a French professor in the fish restaurant on the opposite bank; and here, sick in my cupboard room at the Pensão, watching the slowly moving bugs, like small ripe strawberries lazily creeping among the cracks in the plaster; and here in Nazaree, among the fisher-folk *en fête*, listening to a burly man with a green paper cap who sings songs full of sacred imagery to the riotous accompaniment of his accordion; and here in the low dance-halls, where ship-wrecked Scandinavian sailors pick up polyglot tarts; and here swimming in the chilly Atlantic waters; and here eating sugar-cakes in the tea-shops, among the little, overstuffed Portuguese women and the stranded Irish governesses and the ruined Jewish industrialists.

And here in the Consulate queue, waiting for my daily ration of ten escudos. The queue is a little different each day, yet always the same. Faces flash in and flash out, like fish glimpsed among the waves. Often I recognize one of them: this one had been a white blob on dirty straw in Limoges; this one had stared at me with impersonal rage from a gutter in Toulouse; this one had been offered to the sea, projecting itself madly across the Mediterranean from the harbour wall in Marseilles. Faces loom and retreat like the plasma images at that seance once in a house in Bloomsbury and, without any medium to make their claims for them, they insist that they are my brothers and sisters, my mother and father, my grandparents and my ancestors to the fourth and fifth generations. They are like leeches, staking their claims in my blood. When I try to repudiate them, they stare at me with glassy eyes, muttering in strange languages, and when the shadow of the Consul's clerk looms behind the glass door, they stamp on my toe in revenge.

And meanwhile, the heat folds itself around me, the swamp heat of August in Lisbon. Towards midday, rococo walls flower with nightmares, pushing out stems and roots and clutching hands, and high-pitched laughter. The sun whirls like a top among encircling rainbows, the sea becomes a stiff layer of silver plating. The shoals of porpoises hoot upwards towards the sun and crack the sea in their descent. The birds have vanished. Only a crowd of ramshackle youths play half-hearted football upon the beach. And meanwhile, and meanwhile, and meanwhile. . . .

Now the sea has become a great mirror, stretching all the way to America, existing only to hurl the sun's reflection back at the sky. The little bright ships skate back and forth on the polished silver tea-tray of the sea and the sun bounces like a big ball of yellow rubber. A coal-boat edges into the harbour, a sticky black lump to which cling a seething and glutinous mass of flies. The mass of flies quivers, gradually disintegrates, and they are people, tottering down the gangway, swollen purple faces, spindly legs, eyes begging for mercy. Little blue-jowled Portuguese policmen hustle about, sweating; an ambulance drives up, some bored consular clerks arrive to stare and shuffle scraps of rubber-stamped paper.

'*Signal!* . . . *Signal!*' bleats a one-legged newspaper seller, holding out the shiny magazine with its coverful of radiant Nazi youth.

'They positively *rob* you at the exchange,' an Englishwoman complains, boiled in striped washing-silk.

A barefoot fisher-girl dances a shadow fight with an invisible enemy.

Now God is dead.

Did she know what she was saying, that day in her gallery in Montparnasse? Why did she say that? Why christen despair? God had died, or gone bankrupt.

The house without walls; the reservoir without banks; the sea without a shore; the heart without a breast. I am no longer Me. Only a meaningless sprat caught up in Niagara.

Now God is dead.

I was never conscious of the frame of my life until it was broken; nor of its banks until they crumbled and the water seeped away into the sand.

It occurs to me for the first time that I may be of no significance. For the first time I am forced to consider that I may be nothing but a parcel of short-lived atoms, at the mercy of any senseless catastrophe. This new deaf-mute imbecile of a world may freeze or split; it may sprout a mindless fungus of armies; at one moment it may feed, haphazardly, its animal life – at another moment, not. At any rate, that makes sense, I know where I am now. It makes more sense than trying to sweep the water back into the reservoir whose walls have crumbled away. It makes a mere laughing-stock of the Polish Jews who take themselves so seriously and have probably even chattered about free-will. . . .

It makes a laughing-stock of me too. I can't be expected to like that.

Just consider: from the time when I was a small child, I have watched myself grow as though nothing so important and exciting had ever happened in the world before. I believed that when I was born, I had been given an island to explore. No one had ever been there before, and no one would ever go there again. I did not know whether it was a large or a small island, whether it was a bleak, rocky place, covered only with short scrub and gull-droppings; or whether it was full of bright birds and secret ways and pleasure-palaces like those of Kubla Khan. I only knew that I had recognized my island and meant to explore every cranny of it. Each birthday was a step forward, a flag planted in the soil of my own land.

Every thought which formed in my brain seemed to me an absolutely unique event. I had turned the pages of my history book which began at the time of the ancient Britons who painted themselves with woad, and considered that, of all the people in all those centuries, none had known *exactly* that image which had just formed itself in my head, small and sharp and bright, like a tiny picture painted on enamel, or like the window of a church as high as my thumb.

Consider that, when I had picked a white narcissus from the flower-bed on the second terrace of our Somerset garden, it occurred to me that it was an object of sacred significance. No one before me, and no one ever again, would hold just that flower, would see the sun glowing through that exact texture of white petal, or feel exactly that same mingling of terror and joy at the violent, sweet, languid smell which seemed to promise pleasure and pain at which I could not yet guess.

It was one of the flowers of my island.

Well, it seems it was all a mistake. There never was any island. There was just a collection of cells, roughly coagulated in the shape we know as human, which would normally wear out in seventy years or so, but were likely now to become disintegrated very much sooner. The narcissus had presumably been another collection of cells in a different form. As for the no-man's-land on which these two groups had encountered each other, it is impossible, under these new conditions, even to speculate on its nature.

And death? I had thought a great deal about death and believed it to signify the ultimate possession of my island. All

27

explored, all possessed, every centimetre mine for ever. However, it seemed that I had been foolish and that my death would merely mean the unnatural order of the cells of my body returning to their natural chaos. That ditch in the Beauce, where I lay writhing with other cells, was in fact the right place for me. When you come to think of it, it explains a great deal if human existence is an offense against nature. It explains why nature is always trying to get rid of us and why we have to put up such a struggle to maintain the final shape of our beings.

But the trouble is that my island has become a habit and I cannot live anywhere else.

I have created my own climate, built up, stone upon stone, a temple to myself. I am my own monument.

Long ago, when I was a child, I used to pass a monument to The Men of This Village who have Lost their Lives in the Great War. It was built in granite, upon a grassy space on the hill, just opposite the church, and on it they had carved DULCE ET DECORUM EST PRO PATRIA MORI , and the names of ten young men whose faces I had never seen. My monument commemorates war and peace, joy and pain, a gradual growing, the landscapes of Europe, words, songs, caresses. It commemorates everything that has gone to the slow unfolding of my life. It was built and is for ever growing higher and stronger, in the belief that I am of immense importance, and that everyone around me is of immense importance. It is built in the belief that every second of my life has been the reflection of a terrible and mysterious life which enfolds it as the sea enfolds an island. It is built in the belief that the slightest word or action has not only great significance but many great significances. That a single syllable may be the auditory representation of the most banal of objects or, pronounced in a different key, may become possessed of an occult power sufficient to wrench soul from body. That horror and beauty and love and death are only different aspects of a whole. That there is a whole. That every object or every sensation is only part of the whole object or the whole sensation.

And now it occurs to me to write upon the monument which

I have raised to myself those same words which a village stone-mason carved laboriously, many years ago, upon the granite of a Somerset war memorial. *Dulce et decorum est. . .* With this difference. I do not find it sweet or fitting to die for any of the lands which are named upon the map of the world, and to none of which I wholly belong. *Dulce et decorum est* to know and possess my island, and for every man to know and possess his own island.

III

Somewhere there must be a diary, a big, square exercise book with blank pages – none of those ruled lines that grab one's thoughts and lead them firmly in the right direction, with no wavering allowed, nor any of those words that droop because one is tired or discouraged, or bound upward in an undisciplined way because they prolong an moment of exultation. If I had that diary with me now – it came from the big stationer's shop in Charing Cross Road – if I had it here to read and copy from, I should know just how I felt at certain moments I must surely have recorded. For instance: watching from the roof of the Free French G.H.Q. in Carlton Gardens two planes fighting each other in the sky, little spurts of flame bursting from one, then another, then one of them suddenly wrapped in fire, plunging down and down. . . Which was it? All of us (up there on the roof when we should have been down in the shelter) behaved like a well-trained chorus. Breath held. A shout from Corporal Vanaert, 'It's theirs!' Breath noisily exhaled. A cheer. Jumping up and down, clapping our hands. I behaved exactly like everyone else, felt exactly like everyone else. Only when the flames had disappeared into the ground somewhere in the outer suburbs, I (we?) thought of the young crew hurtling downward, bodies flaming in the flaming plane. . . there was just an instant's silence, then the lieutenant said, 'Better get back to work.'

I forget when the old exercise-book disappeared. If it was during the careful, saving days, it probably got pulped down and re-emerged covered with newsprint or as a wrapper for prime pork sausages. If it was around a bit longer, I suppose it just disintegrated among the sodden mass in some waste-tip.

So now there are only scraps that have survived in stored suitcases, scribblings that come to light at unexpected moments, and above all, there are passages printed on the tissue of memory: all far less coherent than the entries in the tall account book which happened to be lying about on the day I decided to start recording my dreams. That ledger has come through everything. It turns up from wherever it was bundled away before a journey, before a move to some new home. A bad shape, too tall to be fitted in with paperbacks, unshelvable, always there, insisting I add yet another entry in the log-book of my night-time voyages.

JOURNAL
(Probably November 1940 and following months)

This wartime London is a newly-created city, nothing like the grey, sober town I knew during pre-war visits. A city reinvented by all these French, Czechs, Poles, Dutch, Norwegians and so on, who dash about in unrecognizable uniforms, rows of medals on their chests, setting up clubs, creating restaurants serving un-English food, filling the foggy air with strange sounds. I think this has become above all a violent town, not just because of the blitz, but because of the colour and movement, the music, the dancing, the strange uniforms and strange languages, the buildings that burst suddenly into flames, rain down bricks and rafters, send splintered glass singing through the air.

One sees only young, vigorous people here. The old and the children have gone to the country. Everyone is busy at some kind of war-work, then fire-watching on the roofs at night, or dancing in the new clubs. A tremendous current of energy seems to flow through the city and no one ever admits to being tired. There is not much talk about the war. I think everyone feels that what will happen will happen. Meanwhile, we live from day to day, almost from minute to minute.

I am still a stranger here, knowing only a few people, most of them cast up like myself from the French shipwreck. Once a week, I get a news-sheet with lists of arrivals and names of people trying to get in touch with their families. A few familiar

31

names, meetings, then off they go to the Hebrides or wherever their training camps are located.

The Chiswick Eyot has disappeared once more under the water – just some tips of marsh-grass or pink ragwort showing above the gently-moving, silvery surface. This happens once a day when the tide sweeps up from the Estuary. A few days ago, it was so high that the Mall was flooded. Swans sailed by my window, turning their heads very slowly as they passed, as if listening to the music playing on my gramophone. In the afternoon a barge arrived, punted by two boy-scouts, who enquired whether we wanted to be rescued.

For some reason, it made me feel deeply happy to be cut off from the world in this pale, grey waste of water and then to slip on to the solid little raft and glide away to land. I think this must have something to do with the passage between sleeping and waking. I have no time now to reflect on this.

Last night the German planes zoomed up the Thames and dropped fire-bombs on the wharfs near Dukes Meadows. These must have been used as an oil depot, for they blazed up at once and in a few moments the water was covered with a sheet of burning oil. Then the boats at the quayside broke their moorings and the high wind sent them tearing down towards Hammersmith Bridge, shooting flames into the sky. We watched this great wall of fire rushing past our windows, driven by the wind. A crimson river and the flames reflected in the sky so that it looked like a sheet of red-hot metal. For a moment I had a sort of hallucination, as if I were part of the scene, as if I had been caught up in the blood-stream of some giant and was flowing through his veins. Then the firemen came hammering on our door, shouting to us to get ready to evacuate. But the oil was beginning to burn itself out and the flames died down, as if they were being sucked into the river.

When it was safe to go out, we filled thermos flasks with tea and wheeled them on our bicycles, through a foul reek of burnt oil, to the firemen still working at the wharves.

Remembering:

My days belonged to the Free French in
Carlton Gardens. The thrill of that voice I heard crackling out
of a wireless set in Aubusson was still in my ears when I came
to them. I was ready to die for General de Gaulle and enjoyed
imagining various heroic but painless ways in which I might
do so. But I never even glimpsed him. I was just given a sec-
retarial job in the office of an ambiguous person called Com-
mandant Howard.

Everything in our department was very secret. People came
and went mysteriously; doors were for ever being locked and
unlocked. When a specially mysterious visitor arrived I was
sent downstairs to wait in the drivers' room. These drivers
were English girls in khaki uniforms, with impeccable hair-dos
and loud, shopping voices. They lounged, waiting for orders
to drive somebody somewhere, telling each other stories about
evenings out with their various generals and colonels. They
knew all the gossip, all about the feuds and quarrels between
officers who called themselves by the names of Paris metro-sta-
tions: Bienvenue, Vavin, or Passy, who was the head spy. All
this gossip whiled away the hours and I heard it in snatches,
waiting for the telephone to ring and tell me I was allowed
back in the office.

I felt happier in the press section, where I went to take
morning coffee with my friend Mima Kerr. It was run by
Maurice Schumann, a nice, ugly, friendly man who had been
one of the first French to answer the call of de Gaulle.* He
was a converted Jew who had become a devout Catholic, but
had trouble with his conscience on account of an uncontrolla-
bly amorous nature. Some of the drivers had succumbed to
his charm and told giggly stories about poor Maurice's laments

* Maurice Schumann was the Chief Official Broadcaster in the BBC French
Service, 1940-44, then a Liaison Officer with the Allied Expeditionary
Forces at the end of the war. He became a member of de Gaulle's 'provisional
consultative Assembly', had a brilliant career in politics and diplomacy, and
is now a member of the French Academy – C.M.

over his own back-slidings. It was he who broadcast each evening to France, starting with: 'Honneur et patrie, voici la France libre', pronounced in a thrilling voice designed to stir up heroism. Once he took me with him to Bush House. I sat in the studio and listened while he stood in his battle-dress, speaking directly to France, urging the French to resist the occupants, to kill German soldiers. Afterwards, messages went out over the air: 'Madeleine sends kisses to Arthur', 'There is blackberry jam for breakfast'. Somewhere out there, people were listening and understanding, sharpening knives or loading pistols. I thought suddenly, for no reason at all, of a little plumber who had once come to mend a burst pipe in the flat over Jeanne Bucher's gallery. Perhaps he was listening, eager or frightened, knowing there was something he must do. But what would happen to him afterwards?

This formless life through which I drifted rather suited my current mood, but in my office I became more and more ill-at-ease. Howard and his two accolytes, Colin and Jobez, were suspicious of me. They watched me, sometimes secretly from beneath lowered eyelids, sometimes with hard, hostile stares. Did they think I was making reports to the British? Or to Admiral Muselier, their deadly enemy? Or had I betrayed in some way a secret of which I had no knowledge? Guilt invaded me. When Howard left on his desk a document headed 'Secret' in red ink, I felt something was expected of me. People were watching me, perhaps waiting for me to photograph it with some special kind of camera.

Instead, I went home and telephoned that I was ill and could not return.

Lying in bed day after day, paralysed by inexplicable fatigue that attacked me without warning, like a blow from a fist or a heavy blanket wrapping itself around me and immobilizing me. The first time it happened, a little German refugee doctor with a face like a crumpled cabbage came and sat by my bed for an hour, quoting Mandelstam. Then he gave me an injection of some pink stuff which made me feel much worse. After

34

that I just lay and listened to the river-sounds: police-barges chugging along, on the look-out for floating mines or suicides; people hoeing in the little riverside gardens which disappeared quite often under water; seagulls up from the estuary, squawking and dipping for thrown bread; the heavy flapping of swans' wings.

How was it that Dylan Thomas was there one day sitting on the edge of my bed, hugging his knees, talking?* Someone must have brought him, then left us alone to talk. Anyway, there he was, small and cherubic, snub-nosed, curly daffodil-yellow hair and rather globulous light-brown eyes. A rich, fruity voice with hardly a trace of Welsh accent. He began to talk at once about Love, saying it was the only thing which gave meaning to life, yet that he found it terrible and threatening. I knew he was married to an Irish girl and understood that she brought problems.

He gazed at me then with a kind, pitying look and said: 'I hope you are not very ill. I know you have tuberculosis like myself. At least it has kept me out of the Army.'

I wonder why he thought I had tuberculosis? The disease was still prevalent in those days and difficult to cure, but it had a sort of poetical, pathetic prestige, perhaps because Keats had died of it. However, I had been told by Julian Trevelyan,† who knew Dylan well, that he had been exempted for flat feet.

He had brought me a small volume of his poems. Death-obsessed poetry, full of romantic pathos, yet with sudden, revealing gleams of realism. A dead woman, an aunt, I think: 'And sculptured Ann is seventy years of stone.' This brought a very distant memory of narrow streets and small, hostile grey houses, windows guarded by heavy lace, and always the sound of the cataract crashing in pale-mauve hills beyond,

---

* Dylan Thomas (1914-53) at this point had published two collections, *18 Poems* (1934) and *25 Poems* (1936), and a volume of short stories, *Portrait of the Artist as a Young Dog* (1940).
† Julian Trevelyan (b. 1910), painter and etcher, then married to Ursula Darwin (subsequently to Mary Fedden).

though in the poem there was just a dead woman lying in a room with a stuffed fox and a fern.

The publishing house of Routledge, Kegan Paul was situated then in Carter Lane, at the edge of the City, in an area made desolate by bombs. I had imagined a stately building and smart, snappy secretaries, but the house was reassuring in its Dickensian grime. Books piled in the entry had apparently survived a recent blitz. The receptionist was fat and elderly. The Franklin brothers, directors of the firm, were known as Mr Norman and Mr Colin, which suggested ordinary human beings. Mine was Mr Colin. He was youngish, with round spectacles and an avuncular manner. He said: 'Why don't you write a book for us?'

I could not imagine doing such a thing. A few of my poems had appeared in literary magazines and there had been a couple of short stories, signed with a pseudonym, because the thought of seeing my name in print had intimidated me. A book suggested the sort of sustained effort for which I felt ill-prepared. 'Write everything down just as you remember it,' said Colin Franklin. He was generous enough to give me an advance, but prudent enough to pay it in instalments, on receipt of manuscript chapters.

I bought a ream of typing paper and sat by my gas fire, calculating how many pages I should have to fill before there were enough of them to make a book. The pile of paper seemed enormous and every page would have to be covered with writing. I knew that long before I got to the last page I would have nothing left to say. Already I had nothing to say that could possibly interest anyone else. It was one thing to tell stories of those adventures in France, but quite another to write them down. They would fall flat, lose all the flavour I had given them – imprudently, I was beginning to think – in the telling. I had raised false hopes. I had been doing the very thing I had been so constantly warned against at home and at school: I had been showing off, and so effectively that it had even reached the ears of Mr Colin in his venerable publishing house. Now it was too late to withdraw.

So I wrote. Mist and rain veiled the river. Sometimes the Eyot was visible, sometimes not. Days grew shorter. At teatime we drew blinds, not a chink of light must be shown. Enemy planes whirred overhead; anti-aircraft guns spluttered. I lived two lives similtaneously. At one moment I was back on some French road, dizzy with sun, begging a glass of water from a suspicious peasant woman, or leaning on a parapet in Marseilles, gazing out at the schooner which would perhaps carry me to Egypt. At the next, I was out in the dark street, ready with my sand-bag because fire bombs were dropping in the district. Somewhere between the two, there was the sort of daily life which had existed before the war and would presumably carry on when it was over. It crowded in on me, made claims which were mostly ignored. Dirty plates piled up in the kitchen; laundry accumulated; dishes burned in the oven. Eveything was put off, or not done at all. I was absorbed in this difficult yet strangely exhilarating business of writing a book.

Remembering:

How I went alone one evening to Olwen Pike's *Petit Club français*. The Free French and a lot of others used to meet there in the evenings to drink and sometimes to dance. They loved Olwen because she created a cozy, English atmosphere, yet one felt at the same time that France was not far off. Maurice Schumann was there, and Elena de la Souchère, a half-Spanish journalist, who looked like one of those androgenous young saints one sees in the stained-glass windows of medieval churches. I felt drowsy and contented, happy because my book had appeared* and Durrant's Press-Cutting Service sent clippings with kindly notices from the

---

* This was an account of my journey through France. Routledge published it in 1941 and insisted on the title *I Came Out of France*. I wanted 'Ship of France', from Walt Whitman's 'O star, O ship of France, beat back and battered long' – C.M.

critics. A young Frenchman came to my table, asked if he might join me. He wore civilian clothes and muttered a name I was not meant to catch. This was usual at that time when so many people were still a little embarrassed by names to which they had not yet become accustomed.

We talked till Olwen began to clear tables and shoo clients away. He offered to see me home. It was late and the streets very quiet. There had been only a short air-raid earlier in the evening; now there were just a few fire-watchers talking and smoking in their huts, and sometimes a group of people laughing and gossiping on the pavement. We talked about ourselves and asked each other questions. I asked him where he was stationed and he said, 'I have only just arrived. Yesterday I was still in France.'

I wondered for a moment if he could be telling the truth. For months, men had been arriving from Britanny or Lisbon, but for quite a long time now these escape-routes had been cut off. I was just about to ask, when I realized it would be indiscreet to do so.

A little later he said, 'I must not tell you my real name. Will you just call me Yves?' Then he began telling me about Paris, where he had been only one day earlier. He told me how sad and dull everything had become, how people had to queue for food and often there were only turnips to buy, and how the streets were empty after curfew and there was no sound to be heard except the boots of German patrols ringing on the pavements.

When we parted he said, 'I am afraid we shall not meet again.' But I had guessed already that he was one of the men who were organizing the underground resistance in France,* one of those to whom the Free French sent out cryptic messages each evening.

---

* Many years later, I discovered by pure chance his real name. He was Yvon Morandat, one of the most important figures in the Resistance. De Gaulle had sent for him to discuss the unification of the different Resistance groups. After the war he played a leading role in the French Labour Movement. He died in 1983 – C.M.

Lying in bed, I tried to imagine Paris as Yves had described it, but soon I began to doze and then it seemed to me that I was in the boulevard St Michel, walking up from the Seine towards the Luxembourg Gardens. It was warm and the sun shone on the bright dresses of women sitting on the café terraces. There was a smell of lilac. A man was singing in front of the Café de Cluny, holding out his hat for people to toss coins. He was singing *Plaisir d'Amour*. I heard it quite distinctly, the notes sweet and pure in the clear air. Then I saw Yves walking towards me. He did not stop or speak but just smiled in a provocative, challenging sort of way. I turned and ran after him and caught his arm. I said: 'You were telling me lies. Everything is just the same.'

I woke because the sirens were sounding. There was another air-raid, but nothing much happening, only a few dull thuds away to the east. I got up and fetched my dream-diary and began to note my dream while it was still fresh in my mind. I wanted to write about the state of pure happiness I had experienced as I stood outside the Café de Cluny and listened to a man singing *Plaisir d' Amour*: a happiness so intense that it had brought tears to my eyes; my cheeks were still wet. I wanted to explain this. I wanted the whole small scene to live on the page, exactly as it had existed for a moment before I awoke. I tried; there was nothing but a flat statement. It was at that exact moment, I think, that I realized that the power of words is limited and there are things which cannot be said, states which exist only in dreams, or perhaps at the highest peak of love, and for which there is no corresponding language. The flying-dream, for instance: drifting through the air, arms stretched out like wings, sometimes gliding smooth and high above fields and woods, born up by unfelt air, sometimes swooping low, almost brushing against tree-tips, then up again, in slow, lazy loops, up to the sky. A sensation of pure bliss belonging to some place or dimension which has no counterpart in the waking world and in which language becomes meaningless. Nor, come to think of it, can language really cope with the terror of certain nightmares – the charging bull, the maddened horse with its gaping, scarlet throat and its yellow, dripping fangs. . .

Reflecting on this as I lay waiting for the all-clear sound, I realized that it was something which must be accepted. I had begun by now to think of myself as a writer; I had believed that words would be my instrument, enabling me to tell everything about myself, everything I thought and felt, and about an image of the world which belonged solely to me. I had thought too that in time I should become able to tell about other people and how they felt, and perhaps about each of their worlds. Now, it appeared that this would never be possilbe. There would always be a region of unsayable things, an enfenced area, with a great notice-board saying: 'Writers not admitted.'   Later, I tried to remember bits of poetry which came nearest to saying at least something about dream-delight: 'A green thought in a green shade', perhaps? Or that poem by Francis Thomson:

It was a mazeful wonder,
Thrice three times it was enwalled
With an emerald,
Sealèd so asunder
All the birds in middle air
Hung adream, their music thralled. . .

This really means nothing at all, or at least doesn't make sense, which is perhaps the reason why it comes almost near to saying what cannot be said. The pleasure-grounds of Kubla Khan too – but there was a dose of opium in that ink.

'Yves', who I had known for only a few hours, led me to Ignace Legrand, who remained my friend till his death. A letter came from him asking me to contribute an article to a special 'Hommage to France' number of the review *Aguedal*. I wrote about that stroll through night-time London and its dream-sequel, and was invited to Forest Hill, where the Legrands lived since their escape from France.

Thinking of Ignace Legrand sends me searching my book-shelves for his novels. The pre-war paper has taken on a yellowish tinge; pages have jagged edges because in those days one had to cut them before reading. I must have sliced them impatiently or hacked at them with the edge of a postcard. Words flowing out in long, long paragraphs, as though he has more to say than he can easily tell; often difficult to read, because his way of seeing life is so unlike that of anyone else. One is apt to come adrift half way down a page.

Ignace talked in the same way as he wrote, and here he is, clear in my mind, just as I knew him. Very tall, a beautiful, dreamy face set in an expression of determined sorrow – a face resembling both halves of that unlikely couple who were his parents: Russian Jew and Gascon peasant. Innocent and egotistic as a child. Romantic, refusing to admit the belittling realities of life. An inward-looking gaze that does not understand, or misunderstands, the outside world. Lunching with him and Irène in the little French restaurant in Greek Street he begins to talk about prostitutes, whom he considers as saint-like women devoted to the comfort of suffering mankind, despised and rejected as the holy must always be. Carried away by his own fervour, talking on and on in loud, thrilling accents, while the neighbouring tables listen in shocked silence.

He worships England and everything English in the same indiscriminate way. Everything England does is right; everything France does is wrong. He likes to think the Free French want to ban his books. But the Free French have not read them.

Irène: tiny, like a little bright bird, also half-Jewish, the other half French aristocrat. Ignace's volubility is such that she seldom gets a chance to speak. He uses her shamelessly to fetch and carry for him, but there is a definite personality beneath the meek exterior. Nadia, their daughter, has dark, dreamy eyes like her father's. Something there is waiting to make itself felt.

The Trevelyans held a party in their disused wharf which jutted into the Thames, so that one had the impression of being in a boat and that the place might begin gently rocking on the tide.

A lot of Julian's painting on the walls and canvasses by John Banting, Graham Sutherland and some English Surrealists who seemed to me imitative, as if they were doing something they thought they ought to be doing.

Julian: one of our nearest neighbours, tall and gangling with an unhappy face which looked as it it had been carved out of a chunk of wood. Very popular in the art world, but somehow making me uneasy, perhaps because those very light eyes never seemed quite to focus on anything. Ursula a sort of Earth-Mother figure serving drinks and being nice to everyone, though I could see she would sooner have been somewhere else. A lot of writers and artists: William Empson, keeping aloof and cultivating his mandarin image; George Barker too, who sometimes joined us on Sunday mornings at the Black Bull when he swooped down on Chiswick to stay with Elizabeth.* I once went to their house, which was permeated with Elizabeth's distraught tension. Barker has the most beautiful blue eyes.

Dylan, with his wife Caitlin. Remembered now as pretty, though running a little to fat, with a lot of uncombed yellow hair. Dylan and I sitting quietly in a corner. One heard stories about wild drinking and uncouth behaviour. True perhaps, but I always saw him sober and polite. I surely noted our conversation. The actual words and phrases are gone but their flavour remains. Talking a bit about poetry and a bit about life and telling each other some funny stories. Me, happy discovering he liked several of the things I liked and which sophisticated people are not supposed to like – such as the novels of John Buchan and films where you know at once which are the goodies and the baddies. We were enjoying ourselves quietly when Caitlin came up behind me and stubbed her cigarette down on my hand. I have sometimes wondered since if so

---

* William Empson (1906-1985), poet and critic; George Barker (b. 1913), poet, then recently returned from America (*Eros in Dogma*, 1944); Elizabeth Smart (1913-1986), author of *By Grand Central Station I Sat Down and Wept* (1945).

irrational an act can really have happened, but I am sure it did. Was she drunk? She showed no signs of it, or did she seem to think she had done anything unusual. She just said, 'Hullo,' and walked away to talk to someone else. Dylan looked only a little embarrassed and not at all surprised.

Nancy Cunard: talking with tremendous volubility to some French sailors in York Minster, where we had our rendez-vous.* About fifty, I suppose – very thin, with a small delicate face like a faded flower; beautiful in an ethereal way, yet a little grotesque because of the over-painted eyes and hair cut short in the style of the 1920s, with kiss-curls plastered on the cheeks. We recognized each other at once, no need for intro-ductions. She: 'Come here. Quick. We must talk. This is Jean-François, he came over in a fishing-boat as soon as he heard the de Gaulle broadcast. Jean-François, this is Cecily. She has written the most beautiful poem for my volume of "Poems for France".'
    Me: 'But I haven't. . .'
    She: 'But you will, my dear. You will.'

We walked to Charlotte Street. Both quick, springy walkers. She told me about her house in Normandy, about the hand-press she used to print texts too avant-garde for the ordinary run of publishers. What has happened to the press, the manus-cripts, the rare volumes, her collection of ivory bracelets? She talks with great intensity, sure I will agree with everything she says, or perhaps daring me not to agree. Phrases full of unex-pected, bizarre images, such as I sometimes heard from the Surrealists who used to call at Henry Miller's studio. A lot of questions about the Spaniards I met in Toulouse. Why are the English so indifferent about Spain, about everything? All the time she was speaking, I could feel her contained rage, like a saucepan about to boil over.

* Nancy Cunard (1896-1965), poet, translator and publisher; editor of the important anthology *Negro*, biographer of Norman Douglas.

I hadn't a poem about France, had written nothing of the sort but strangely, as soon as I got home, I did so. I suppose it was because we had talked for so long about France that I had a sudden, vivid vision of the man who laughed in that café somewhere beyond Nantes, and the people dragging themselves along the sunlit roads, and the smell of clover. It all came out in a rush in quite a classical form, I rather liked it, and she liked it too. It went:

A man in the café laughed and said: The war is done.
The moment froze and joined the starry way
Of clear immutable things men do and say
That spin in whirling history round a tired sun.

Along the roads the tired people lay,
Death's feet were quiet in a sky of indigo,
It seemed an old song of Touraine from long ago
Still lingered in that centuries-old evening, fragile and gay.

The chequered map of France beneath our feet
Unrolled itself day after clover-smelling azure day,
Incarnate Summer's ultimate and proud display
Before she laid her corn and birds and flowers down in
    defeat.

Nancy and I became friends, meeting most often by chance, in unexpected places. Each time we met, I felt the same little jolt of excitement, a quickening of life's tempo. With Nancy, people and things shifted into new perspectives. One found oneself in a world of violent and generally unreasoning loves and hates, of tremendous partisanships and at the same time of a fantasy which transformed a landscape, an underdog, or whatever was preoccupying her at that moment into something poetical, illogical and debonair. Nancy created her own climate and shared it, like everything she had, with reckless generosity.

JOURNAL
(Strange that, while the diary has long since disappeared, there

remains an angrily crushed-up, torn-out page, full of the frustration of having nothing to say about what was, after all, an important occasion.)

This afternoon, Barbara Barclay-Carter took me to have tea with T.S. Eliot in his little office at Faber's. Unused to meeting famous people, I was intimidated, sure that I should be tongue-tied and might quite probably spill my tea.

T.S.E. . . . . tall and what is called 'perfectly tailored'. A pale, unmoving face on which is fixed a small, courteous smile. I had the feeling that I had no right to be there and that he, with exquisite courtesy, was wondering why I had come. Barbara had told me he wanted to meet me, but my own guess is that he just said he wouldn't mind doing so.

Windows patched up with cardboard; a pile of plaster-powdered books in the corner; table laid with the snowiest of tablecloths, some nice Georgian silver and a covered dish of muffins. Barbara talking earnestly about *People and Freedom*, to which she hopes he will contribute an article, and about her beloved Don Sturzo.* T.S.E. said he had read my book, and some poems. Asked me about the project for *A Mirror for French Poetry*, about which he seems to have heard from Herbert Read.† The conversation had not really got going when the sirens started, then the raid was on us immediately, aimed, apparently, bang at Russell Square. Explosions coming nearer and nearer, anti-aircraft guns pounding away, and now and

* Don Sturzo (1871-1959) was an anti-Fascist priest, founder of the Italian Christian-Democratic Party. Exiled from Mussolini's Italy, he had been living in London before the war and had founded a monthly journal entitled *People and Freedom* to support his ideal of a democratic, slightly left-wing Catholicism. It was edited by his friend and disciple Barbara Barclay-Carter, a specialist on Dante, who died in 1950. I contributed a regular feature under the pen-name 'Rhiannon' – C.M.

† An anthology of French verse from 1840-1940, with translations by English poets who seemed to me to be especially akin to them. It was published by Routledge in 1947 and, since reliable texts were hard to come by at the time, it contained a prodigious number of misprints and mistakes. I corrected these for the American edition, published in 1969 by Books for Libraries Press (New York) – C.M.

then the nasty sound of crumpling buildings. Barbara growing paler and paler. The table was oak, fairly solid; I thought of diving beneath it for shelter. As for Eliot, he remained totally impervious. He just sat there, pouring tea, turning that small, polite smile on each of us in turn. Finally one of the remaining window-panes broke inward, showering glass on the floor, but he just gave a little, annoyed click with his tongue and passed the muffins.

Now I remember more about the bangs than about our talk. Maybe profound and important things were said, but all I recall is: 'A little milk? Or do you prefer lemon?' Somewhere Laforgue and Saint-John Perse were mentioned, but the end of each sentence was drowned in the surrounding clatter.

The whole world seemed to be in London during those years. Governments in exile, and exiles forming governments; imaginary frontiers drawn up; rival factions furiously plotting; the Hapsburg Empire reconstituted and destroyed again. Russia had come into the war and was battling for Stalingrad. Stalin was everybody's hero, and it would have been in the worst of taste to mention the Soviet-German pact. De Gaulle was in Algiers, and my ex-colleagues Howard, Colin and Jobez had been arrested, and were said to be languishing in the Tower of London. The world was a vast jigsaw puzzle which sometimes appeared to be taking shape, but there were always missing pieces and no pattern was ever revealed.

The Free French, Free Czechoslovaks, Free Poles and so on each had their own club, their own library, their own canteen. The worse the news, the more parties they gave. Tin helmets left in the cloakrooms; gramophones playing national folk-music; buffets set with whatever could be cooked out of war-time rations. Madame Hubert Ripka* made penny-sized omelettes from powdered egg, sprinkled them with paprika and set them on canapés made from flour and water. One of the Polish Government ladies discovered tinned vine-leaves in

*Wife of Hubert Ripka, leading member of the Czech Government in exile.

a Dean Street store, and stuffed them with something into the nature of which it was better not to inquire. The Free Belgians, somewhere near Eaton Square, were inclined to bicker over the rather ambivalent role of their King, who had returned to Belgium and married a beautiful girl from Flanders. They ran a French-language magazine called *Messages*. Monsieur Weyemberg – the editor, I think – sometimes gave parties where squares of stale Belgian chocolate were washed down with beer, which arrived in great quantities by some mysterious route. He was a veteran of the First World War, during which both his legs had been blown off. They had been replaced by rather clumsy prostheses, and he stumped among his guests, shy and elderly, begging them to write articles on English poets who had struck his fancy. Queen Wilhelmina of the Netherlands was in London, but she lived austerely and was seldom seen in public, though she was said to serve coffee with her own hands to a favoured few.

My own favourite was the Free Hungarian Club in Connaught Square. Catherine Karolyi reigned there, her soft-slurred voice pleading, 'Please dear so-and-so, will you do something for me?' and people scurried to do whatever she wanted – such as washing up the tea-cups for a new round of visitors.

Her beauty had a special quality, which seemed to come from far away and long ago; eyes like leaves, green and elongated. For the last thousand years or so, and up to 1918, her family had owned a large part of Hungary, and of its population at the same time. She and Michael lived in one of those little Georgian houses in Hampstead, where she cooked and cleaned with queenly good humour. But I suspected that Genghis Khan still lurked in some deep part of her subconscious. If so, she rejected him vigorously and remembered proudly that she had been known throughout Austria-Hungary as 'the Red Countess'.

There was a party at the Free Hungarian Club to celebrate Michael Karolyi's seventieth birthday. I remember him as very tall, with a long, hatchet face recalling the portraits of certain Hapsburgs. His cleft palate made him hard to understand, but

Michael Karolyi

that had not prevented him from rousing a rebellion in his country, freeing her from the domination of Austria and becoming first President of the Hungarian Republic. He made a little speech that evening, saying that he had failed in all he had dreamed of doing, but that he had not lost hope. The war would end; someone, even if it was not himself, would go back to Budapest to re-establish democracy. Catherine raised her glass defiantly, her green eyes flashing, refusing to admit defeat. Several emotional Hungarian eyes brimmed with tears.

All of us threw bridges across time into a future where there was as yet no solid anchorage. All of us, from whatever country we came, knew that however the war might end, nothing would ever be the same again. Britain was moving too, as fast as those imagined countries across the Channel that were waitng to become real. I understood this on the day of my interview with a large woman in khaki, with pips on her shoulders. She told me about the Army Bureau of Current Affairs and invited me to join a panel of civilian lecturers. 'We want the working classes to learn to think and express themselves,' she said. The Army was to be her laboratory. Men home on rest periods from the Eighth Army were to listen to talks on subjects of general interest, then be asked to give their opinions. 'They'll be shy,' she said, frowning in sympathy for my future struggles. 'You must try to get them to talk. It's a question of giving them confidence, making them feel you're interested in what they have to say.'

Rain curtained the windows as the train dragged through the soaking Home County countryside. Barracks were hastily put up in what had once been a wood. Felled trees lay about; a hurriedly tarmacked road scarred a field. A huddle of jeeps was guarded by a sentry whose macintosh cape dripped with rain. Stiff with terror, I confronted a roomful of large khaki-clad men with the bronze of the Libyan sun still on their faces. They listened, not a muscle moving, not a flicker of the eyes, while I talked for ten minutes, just as I had been told to do, working through the guide-points in my booklet. 'Men and

Women: are they equal?' was the subject, I think. Then, swallowing hard: 'Now what do you yourselves think about all this?'

Several of them instantly started talking all at once and in what I took to be a foreign language. No one had warned me; the ABCA booklet gave no hint of how to behave. I could only point at someone in the first row and ask: 'Now what do *you* think about what has just been said?' He told me what he thought, then several others broke in, clamouring to give incomprehensible opinions. They talked on and I stood, smiling and nodding, till a silent officer at the back of the room rose and started a round of applause. Afterwards, the officers revived me with strong tea in their mess. The Colonel said: 'Didn't anyone tell you? They come from Glasgow. Och, someone might have warned ye.'

Discussions spread like wildfire through the Army, then into the ordnance factories. People who had never been asked for their opinions found themselves talking and being listened to. We discussed the declining birth-rate; asked 'Is parliamentary democracy right for everyone?'; 'Should the British remain in India?' and a hundred other things. Everyone, everywhere, seemed to have a mind-picture of what the future was to be.

The organizer for South Wales was Amabel Williams-Ellis, a Strachey, cousin to Lytton, acquainted with Virginia Woolf and the Bloomsbury group. Large, determined and intellectual, she was ready to eat a stodgy breakfast at six a.m. before driving out to speak in factories hidden in folds of the Welsh hills and painted to look like part of the surrounding scenery. I succumbed too easily to fatigue but she was kind and invited me to Port Meirion, lately created by her architect husband. It was a charming place, but unreal, like a picture postcard brought to life.

I was happy and exhausted during those discussing months. I travelled once a week to Cardiff, in trains which grew slower and slower and carriages which grew dirtier and dirtier. I scribbled articles, writing on a pad balanced on my knee, my fountain-pen slashing inky trails across the paper as we lurched over roughly repaired rails. After Cardiff, there were unreliable local trains, and buses which broke down in places inhabited only by sheep. It was fun to alight at an improvised halt, watch soldiers unloading crates for some secret camp and be met by small, dark men with accents which echoed back to my early childhood. I talked to girls in a parachute factory somewhere near Builth Wells. They showed me how to fold the lovely yellow silk and explained how they used scraps to make knickers for themselves. They talked mostly about love. They were young, free of their parents for the first time, experimenting, and generally dismayed at the results. Then I talked to voluble miners in Pontyprydd. They grumbled about the bitter years of the slump. The English were making use of them now, they said, and would throw them back on the dole as soon as the war was over. In the evenings, they persuaded me into the local pub. We drank tepid beer and sang *Cwm Rhondda* and *Calon lân*. I felt warm and cherished, belonging. 'Come on, Miss,' they said, 'another pint and you'll be speaking right way.'

Bridgend was full of jolly, noisy English and Irish girls. The wireless played full blast all day: 'Music while you work' was supposed to step up production, the girls taking up the songs, screaming with laughter at Tommy Handley and the Crazy Gang, but fiddling and hammering at the same time at bits of steel which would become parts of pistols, sten-guns, machine-guns or great cannons to be mounted on tanks out there in the desert.

Hills rose behind the factory. I took an upward path and realized suddenly that this was part of the long range of the Black Mountains and somewhere on the other side was the place where I was born. When I was a child, I used to stare up at the mountains and think that one day I would climb them and discover what lay on the other side. And here I was. The peaks rose up in the same way, just as I remembered them, one behind the other, appearing and disappearing through gauzy veils of changing colours – blue, violet, very pale green

51

and sudden waves of shell pink. The path went only a little way, then there were just stretches of pale, coarse grass scarred with white stones that marked pasturing boundaries. Higher up there were great boulders, piled one on the other, surely erected for some purpose, by those 'Little Dark People' the professor in Cardiff told me about – the race that was here before the Celts and worshipped gods whose names no one knows. It was late in the afternoon and not a sound to be heard, not even a bird singing. The sun was just beginning to go down and a strange, coppery sheen was spreading over the grass. The war and the munitions factory and everything that was going on away in London seemed to have happened long ago, or not at all.

Sitting there, leaning my back against piled boulders, thinking about nothing, just feeling this enveloping peace – a sudden flash of memory, like an electric light switched on in the brain. Standing by our garden wall, my grandmother snipping with her secateurs at the dead heads of roses dripping over the top of the wall. On the other side of the road, a track, at first just sloping, then rising steeply up the craggy side of Skirrid Fawr. A man comes up the road, pauses to speak to my grandmother. I stand between them, imprisoned between two tall bodies. A grey skirt on one side; grey trousers on the other; my head just at the level of the two stomachs. I push angrily at the man. He laughs and turns away and a minute later, there he is, climbing the mountain track. My grandmother turns away and begins to clip again at the roses. I watch the climbing man and there, before my eyes, a miracle occurs. He begins to shrink: now he is no bigger than myself; now he is the size of a dog. I tug at my grandmother's hand, screaming with excitement at my discovery, but she just says: 'It's because he's going further away.'

I noted this memory as soon as I returned, but I was in a hurry because the girls were holding a sing-song in the recreation room. So the scrap of paper had disappeared even before I got back to London. It doesn't matter; the memory is clearer than any words I may have used to tell it.

Maybe this small scene on the slopes of Skirrid explains my longing for travel. Going further away meant at first that, if I could only go far enough, I should become as small as a mouse. Nowadays, I just have a vague feeling that it may perhaps produce some miraculous inner change.

Remembering:

The envelope waiting for me one day when I reached home. A letter from Cyril Connolly and a five-pound note enclosed.* Cyril had appealed earlier to readers of *Horizon* to send a tip to authors of any article they had specially liked (a cunning way of compensating us for his mean rates of pay). Someone had liked my article about Apollinaire and here was my tip.

Off to Cameo Corner – a secret-looking little shop huddled between grimy houses in a street near the British Museum. Artists, writers and such used to linger there, fingering jewels, chatting to old Mr Goode, seldom buying anything.

Mr Goode was there, surrounded by piles of silver and gold. He was gazing into a Persian looking-glass framed in chiselled silver, just slightly twisted to give it a hint of arabesque. He did not greet me but began at once to tell me its story: how he had found it in a flea-market in Cairo, tossed down among a pile of bottles and strings of glass beads. There was an Etruscan ring, bought from a pedlar in a back street in Florence. He fingered it, talking about it in a hypnotic, oriental story-teller's voice which seemed to belong to the Thousand-and-One-Nights. I tried on an Afghan belt, a hands-width wide, studded with huge uncut emeralds; and Persian bracelets of heavy silver, mounting like cuffs nearly to my elbows.

Then he grew suddenly bored and I knew it was time to buy something and leave. There was a pretty pair of antique, ruby-paste earrings, but he became suddenly rapacious and wanted a high price for them. I knew he wanted to bargain,

---

* Cyril Connolly (1903-74), author and journalist; founding editor of *Horizon*, a monthly review of art and literature first issued in January 1940.

but I hadn't the technique. I just held out the five-pound note and told him it was all I had. In the end, he let me have them and said goodbye rather crossly.

Remembering:

My first meeting with Walter Strachan, who became a faithful correspondent. He never throws a letter away and can thus provide me with landmarks for events which have lost their moorings in time and are apt float into the year before, or the year after, or simply to disappear. As he has published a number of these letters, together with those of innumerable friends all over Europe, I have been able to reread them and encounter my own immediate reactions, which are not always those retained in memory.* I suppose they were those most easily communicable, the top layer so to speak.

We met at Bishop's Stortford, where he was then a schoolmaster. . . Sixth-formers sprawled on the sitting-room floor in front of a blazing log fire. . . Talking to them about Mallarmé, reading *Les Fenêtres*. . . I asked them: Was it an example of Mallarmé's morbid pessimism, as their Short History of French Literature told them it was? They caught on at once and a boy with red hair said no, because even if life does seem a bit like a *triste hôpital* from time to time, one can always open the windows and see *les galères d'or belles comme des cygnes/Sur un fleuve de poupre et de parfums dormir*. . .

How we had tea, then inspected the abstract paintings and sculptures Walter collects from France, Italy, Germany. . . and something of Henry Moore's, and something of Ben Nicholson's. . . And all the poets he translates with selfless devotion in any spare time left over from schoolmastering. His own poems are delicate and musical, the best kind of minor poetry.

I wrote to him on 10 March 1945:

Dear Walter Strachan, I got back quite safely, thank you,

---

* See *The Living Curve: letters to W. J. Strachan 1919-1979*, edited by Christopher Hewett (Taranman/Carcanet), 1984.

and very much enjoyed meeting you and your wife, books, tea and talk – it was a really nice afternoon. . . I wish you had been able to come to the Paragon (!) party. It was great fun – frightfully distinguished, with Aragon dressed up as an Englishman *à la française*. He read one of his poems, very badly. I was introduced but couldn't think how to open a conversation so just said *bonjour* and passed on. One of Claudel's daughters was there in an astonishing Paris hat and I had a long talk with her.

A reminder of things inexplicably forgotten, things I must surely have recorded in that lost diary and which I probably saw in a different, younger way. Time has simply swallowed up Aragon's visit, only this letter has survived to prove to me that he came, that I met him briefly and let slip the chance of a talk with this ambiguous personage, who was at once a worshipper of Stalin and a French patriot, a homosexual and the author of passionate love poems addressed to his wife. Yet the little volume of his poems, *Le Crèvecoeur*, remains a vivid memory. It had been printed clandestinely in France and somehow smuggled to London. I remember its arrival and the thrilling sadness it brought me, because it told of the fall of France ('Ma patrie est comme un barque / Qu'abondonnèrent ses hâleurs. . .') and evoked scenes I had shared just a few years earlier. We were still in the middle of the war then. In what corner of our minds, I wonder, do we pick and choose – What to remember – What to forget?

JOURNAL
16 August 1945 (in the train)
On the way back from Rhos. . . Quick jottings before things begin to fade. Tired, dozing now and again, finding myself back in the big Eisteddfod tent. . . Sam Jones translating for me in a loud whisper, a bit resentful because I can't understand for myself. . . Snatches of the *Messiah*. . . a little dark man bounding on to the stage, standing a bit sideways, like a crab, throwing out his chest, bellowing 'Why do the

nations. . .?' The Treorchy Male Choir winning again, unbeatable, with 'Worthy is the Lamb'. . . the bosomy, spectacled woman, the pride of Rhosllanerchrugog, first prize for soprano with 'I know that my Redeemer liveth'. . . and the thin young man, then the little one with a crest of white hair, both drawn up to twice their height, so proud, voices trembling a bit with emotion, reciting their own long, incomprehensible poems.

Then, about half way through, someone hurrying up the main aisle, whispering to the Chief Druid presiding on his carved oak throne (Rev. Rhys-Evans in civilian life). Rev. R-E. ringing a handbell, stopping the Dolgelly choir in its tracks, standing, impressive in his white nightshirt and crown of bay-leaves, announcing that the Japanese have capitulated and the war is really over, for good this time. Everyone was standing, knowing what would happen next. A prayer, of course, in that rich, rolling Welsh that seems specially made for praying and preaching. The whole audience joining in, shouting loud and high to the God of War, then up rose *Cwm Rhondda*, roaring and blasting away, just as it does at rugby matches, fine for unnerving the other side. Sam Jones, a fervent nationalist who never misses a chance to make his point, hisses in my ear: 'You see the way we are here. . . Singing and prrray-ing, us. And what are they doing in London [a portentous pause] . . . Trrunken prrostitutes tancing in Piccadilly. . .'

I noted all these things in the train, coming down from Wrexham. Remembering bits of music, bits of talk – the little girl and her father singing to each other in counterpoint over bacon and eggs in the breakfast tent – all to be worked up for a radio talk next week. At Paddington I went to the bookstall for a morning paper, the first that came to hand. On top of the first page, in the place where the date was usually printed, there was SECOND DAY OF THE ATOMIC AGE, in big, aggressive black lettering.

An unknown, ie-cold future. An atomic Age. No place for Rev. Rhys-Evans, or Sam Jones, or the *Messiah*. No place, I fear, for myself. It's a hot day, but my spine feels like a horrid, chill little icicle running down the middle of my back. I wonder if our most ancient ancestors felt like this as the Stone Age became the Age of Bronze. I wonder if someone felt like this when he saw for the first time a piece of metal being fashioned into some object for future use, or, further and further back, when he first saw fire sparking from a piece of flint. . .?

The *Daily Mail* is keeping it up, shrieking Third, Fourth, Fifth Day. Do they mean to go on with this for ever? I hear it has sent their sales up.

IV

It was midnight when I arrived. The place Denfert Rochereau awash with moonlight. The Lion of Belfort rising out of a pallid ground, white against a white sky. Trees crowned with a lacework of silver branches. No one there; nothing moving. A landscape of pure fantasy, uncharted country, a clean slate upon which anything might be written.

Daytime brought bewilderment. The Paris I had recreated in my dreams was impressed too vividly on my mind to be immediately cast off. It remained with me, a parallel or simultaneous city, like a cliché which has been twice exposed so that a second image is superimposed on the first. I wrote: 'So I am back in Paris – a drab, quarrelsome, undernourished Paris, groping its way painfully back to. . . Back to what? I was going to write "normal", but "normal" just means what we are used to. Perhaps I should get out of the habit of wanting to return anywhere.'

At first I thought: later on, everything will be the same. Next summer, the lime-trees will be in flower again in the Luxembourg Gardens and the smell will drift all the way up here and waft round the old Lion. And the fair will be back on the *place*, with its roundabouts and weight-lifters and bullied child-acrobats, with entranced shop-girls and men-of-letters, all dignity forgotten, astride madly-turning blue pigs. There will be fruit and cheese and wine in the shops in the boulevard d'Orléans, negresses jostling before the cheap out-fitters, sailors lounging round the fruit-stalls, cheap-jacks, and the acid, exciting smell of sweat and dust and fish and oranges. . . And the sad-eyed Algerian will be back, wearing his djellebah, selling peanuts on the terrace of the Dôme; and the little art gallery near the Closerie des Lilas will open again and Rouault's tragic Babylonian king will be back in the window.

Several of these things had already happened, yet nothing was really the same. I rediscovered people and places, just as they used to be, or so it seemed at first, but always there was a change. I understood then that it was time for me to recognize that the past can never be recovered. We rejoin it on the shore, believe for an instant in reunion, the same arms closing around us, the same house opening its door to take us in, yet something is different. Unshared experience has left traces, small scars, signs of subtle alterations. Better to admit that I had strayed into foreign parts and must get my bearings all over again.

In December 1946 I wrote to Walter Strachan:

> You will have read of all our tribulations here in Paris – no gas, electricity, transport, and at one time no water. And very little food, but all is well again for the moment. I manage to work in spite of all this and cooking for four people every day. . . lots of reviewing for [a new review] *Paru*,* an article coming out next month in *Europe* on 'the state of mind of English intellectuals', working on the Mallarmé article for his 50th anniversary number of *Les Lettres*, a long article for *Esprit* and my novel!† Routledge want me to do a travel book on Palestine and the Middle East, but they want me to leave immediately and produce it in about five minutes, so I don't know whether that will be possible. You see I have lots of work but the financial result is lamentable.

> I saw *Le Procès* the other day, adapted from Kafka, mise-en-scène by Jean-Louis Barrault and décor by Gischia. The mise-en-scène and décor were marvellous – so marvellous indeed that one thought about them all the time and Kafka

---

* A monthly literary review, founded and edited by Aimé Patri, a professor of philosophy.
† *Spring's Green Shadow*, published in Britain by MacGibbon Kee in 1952, in New York by Dutton, 1953, and in French translation by Gallimard, 1956.

got swamped in the innumerable 'trucs'. I'm going to see *Les Epiphanies* [by Henri Pichette] because of Gérard Philipe (I suppose you haven't been allowed to see *Le Diable au Corps* in England? I think it's the best film I ever saw but I expect the censor would react violently).

So I wrote to Walter and to other friends in England who have not preserved letters which might have recalled a lot more of the intrusive, time-wasting problems of this resurgent Paris, of tragedies and denunciations, of the furious outburst of creative activity following the years of repression. Had Paris before the war already been as avid of novelty, as furious in its options, as welcoming and as vindictive as it now revealed itself to me? I can only answer that question through other peoples' stories and writings. The 'me' who had listened to the thudding of German guns drawing nearer and nearer to the outlying suburbs, was not the same person who scribbled furiously on scraps of paper, theatre programmes, backs of envelopes, trying to preserve some shreds of a present which dissolved too rapidly into the past to be captured in any other way. Perhaps the chief change was that I had become aware of what was happening.

JOURNAL
Life in St-Germain-des-Prés is vivid and intense, so unlike the drab existence in other quarters that it seems like a state with definite boundaries and its own language and habits. The various cafés around the Square are melting-pots out of which everyone is waiting for some new culture to be born. Rival groups sit for hours on the terrace of the Flore or Deux Magots, refusing to admit each other's existence. The last guard of the Surréalists gathers here – André Breton* with his noble, lion-face; Georges Hugnet; the poet Pierre Perret and some attendant women. Breton declares himself everyone's enemy, everyone has betrayed him. He sits there, not speaking

* André Breton (1896-1966), poet, founder and theorist of the Surrealist movement.

much, gazing out over the Square with sad, beautiful eyes, remembering, I suppose, the great days of the Surrealist Manifesto when he was going to lead his followers deep into the subconscious world and create out of it a life of dream and imagination.

The Existentialists, on the other hand, are certain that the world is already theirs.* Sartre, Simone de Beauvoir, Merleau-Ponty, sit in the shadowy depths of these two favourite cafés, talking, talking, and words like 'phenomenology' and 'empirical existance' drift forward, falling like scattered crumbs of wisdom among would-be disciples who come to gaze and listen. These last are somewhat scruffy and unwashed, because this is now the fashion. They all call themselves Existentialists, but for them Existentialism (whatever that may really be, for I am ignorant about philosophy) means placing a copy of *L'Etre et le Néant* beside one's plate and dancing all night in smoke-filled cellars. Some of the girls manoeuvre to gain Sartre's attention and a few of the prettier ones get themselves invited to dinner or for long initiatory walks along the boulevards. Existentialism is rapidly becoming a way of life rather than a philosophy.

Then there are the Communists, headed by Aragon and Tristan Tzara.† They pause as they approach Breton's table and stare straight through him as if he was a hole in the air, and he stares back at them in the same way. They were once all Surrealists together, then there was one of those huge rows, with hurled furniture and black eyes, followed by pages of vituperation in print.

---

* Jean-Paul Sartre (1905-1980), *L'Etre et le Néant* was published in 1943, and *L'Existentialisme est un humanisme* in 1947; Simone de Beauvoir (1908-86) had published *L'Invitée* (1943), *Le Sang des autres* (1944); with Maurice Merleau-Ponty (1908-1961), the leading French phenomenologist, they founded the review *Les Temps modernes* in 1946.
† Tristan Tzara, who died in 1963, was a Roumanian, inventor of the Dada Movement, dedicated to the destruction of language, society, culture and indeed everything destructible. He had grown considerably calmer by the time I knew him – C.M.

Tristan Tzara is good company and is always friendly to me – perhaps because of Nancy, whose lover he was? is? He is a rather soft, gentle little man, not at all like the furious iconoclast of his reputation, though he sometimes explodes into a rage against anybody who does not totally agree with him. He has explained to me about the Black List. This is drawn up by a committee which examines every book or even article published during the war years for the least hint of collaboration. If such a thing is found, the author's name goes straight on to a list of writers who must not be allowed to write, actors who must not be allowed to act, and so on. Tzara, who spent most of the war with the partisans in some maquis in Central France, is sincere, I think, about this process of 'purification', but denunciation has become a habit here. I am afraid personal ambition and political intrigue play a larger part than one would like to think.

Remembering:

How Roger Blin, Arthur Adamov and some others brought Antonin Artaud on to the stage of the Rose Rouge in the rue du Cherche-Midi.* They stood like warders behind him while he recited poems, or perhaps lectured, inaudibly. Then seized with manic terror, he gibbered, making wild gestures, surely begging for mercy.

Afterwards, I went with Renée Belon, Adamov and some others to the Deux Magots, where we sat till dawn, talking about madness and crime and reality. Adamov believes that true reality can only be attained through the destruction of all accepted values. He talked fervently about Jean Genet, a homosexual thief who spent the war years in Barcelona and writes in startling yet often beautiful language about the underworld of that city and the 'fetid beauty' of its inhabitants. Adamov believes that Genet and Artaud are the true saints of the new age, as Saint John of the Cross was of his time. I

---

* Antonin Artaud (1896-1948), actor, director and dramatic theorist associated with the so-called 'theatre of cruelty'.

reflected, but did not say, that no one thought of putting Saint John on show and charging admission for a view of the dark night of the soul.

Adamov himself is a strange, drugged creature with very deep-set, glowing eyes. His long, bony, equine face is generally distorted in a way which makes him appear to be suffering unexplained torture, but this demonic appearance contrasts with a gentle, and indeed incongruously gentleman-like manner.

JOURNAL

I have only just realized how hungry I nearly always feel – much hungrier than I ever did in London, where food was scarce but arrived in a reassuringly regular way. Here, my temporary ration-book entitles me to about enough to keep a mouse alive, and the shops always seem to have sold out just as I arrive. I hear a lot of talk about the Black Market – indeed, some people talk of little else – but where is it? Apart from a furtive little man selling plums in the rue Boulard last week, I have found no trace of it (the bottom layer of plums was rotten anyway). Then yesterday, R. brought me a panful of cooking oil. I fried all the bread I possessed and ate it to the last crumb. Since then, the taste of crisp, fat-laden bread keeps returning on my tongue, bringing the saliva up into my mouth.

I am caught up in the excitement of this city where everything is happening. I let myself be whirled in the whirlpool. Yet sometimes I feel that there is sadness in all this activity. The shadow of war lies over everything, as if it was not really finished. Surrealists, Existentialists, Communists. . . they are all trying to create the future while their feet still drag in the past. None of us, it seems, is really free. The 'lessons of history', to which the Existentialists so often refer, are too close to be seen in perspective. Perhaps we are living in a sort of interval between past and future.

A little while ago, for instance, I was sitting with G. in the Flore after dining at the Petit-Saint-Benôit. There was a lot of noise, people arguing vehemently, voices sometimes raised to a shout. The door opened and four women came in and stood for a moment searching with their eyes for a free place. At the instant they appeared, all conversation stopped, there was sudden, complete silence. These women were like visitors from outer space, natives of Elsewhere, arriving from some zone of experience none of us had shared. They were not just thin, they were fleshless, made of huddled bones, inside clothes that hung loose from their shoulders. Even more extraordinary, all four were exactly alike. Not alike as sisters might be, but like a single person reproduced in four copies, with hair of the same indeterminate colour and only a slight difference in height to tell them apart. It seemed as if all the individual signs which distinguish one face from another had been sponged away. They walked between the tables in single file, found seats and began talking together in what seemed quite a cheerful way.

Everyone had understood immediately that these were survivors from some German concentration camp.

They came back on three successive evenings. Each time they appeared, there was the same sudden hush, eyes lowered as if something was happening which should not be witnessed. Somehow one felt hostility, as if these women were exposing themselves, doing something indecent. If they had asked for pity, it would have been easier, I suppose. But they didn't want pity. They behaved exactly as if they were alone, talking to each other, laughing sometimes, looking neither to right nor to left. It was as if they had created for themselves a space surrounded by invisible barbed wire. Then one evening they did not appear, and they have not been seen since.

Passing by the Deux Magots last night, there was Nancy, drinking brandy on the terrace with Kay Boyle,* her neat little head crowned by a towering leopard-skin hat.

---

* Kay Boyle (b. 1902), American short-story writer and novelist, who left the USA in 1923 and lived in Europe for forty years.

I joined them and at once there was a programme for me. I must see the Lorca plays: *Noces du Sang* and *La Maison de Bernada Alba*, which will soon be in the theatres; I must meet a group of Spaniards who are plotting against Franco, one of them is a poet whose work Nancy is translating and who will soon be famous; and an anti-Nazi German who was scheming under Hitler's very nose. Her conversation has a special rhythm, is often incoherent. Sentences, rarely finished, remain hanging in the air. Suddenly she was telling us about a journey to Bou Saada: 'Through the window there was yellow, then yellow, then nothing at all. . .' One was with her in the little desert train. There was no need to say any more.

Suddenly, yesterday, a telephone call from Ernest Gimpel. Dinner in the garden of the Club Interallié. The sort of warm, soft night I used to dream of back in London. Ernest very little changed. Both of us careful not to talk about certain things. I enquired about his tank. He drove it into the battles in the North and christened it *L'Indifférent*, like the young man in Boucher's painting, because it never returned his love. He had had to abandon it somewhere near the Belgian frontier. Then he told me about the tennis tournament, somewhere up in the Savoy, where he had played and won under a false name while the Gestapo were hunting for him all over France.

We were both thinking about his father, of course.* Pierre had told me the story back in London. When Ernest was arrested at last and deported, he knew his father had been taken and sent to the same camp. He enquired everywhere, searched through all the huts and in the hospitals, but he had already died.

Ernest's story carried me back to the early days of the war, when nothing seemed to be happening. I used to spend my

---

* René Gimpel (1881-1945), one of the most important art-dealers in France, brother-in-law of Lord Duveen, the English art-dealer.

René Gimpel

afternoons in the flat where Rose Adler had created a circulating library. We sorted books and sent them to bored soldiers on the Maginot Line. There I met René Gimpel, then his three sons. The Gimpel boys were my friends. We went dancing and boating when they came home on leave, but it was their father who really counted. I learned from him more then I have learned from anyone else, before or since. He taught me that art is not merely a matter of the emotions – as I was all too ready to believe – but something which must be understood and analysed. He explained the principles on which the Cathedral of Chartres was erected and the way the great stones of its arches were assembled in the hair-fine balance which would hold them for centuries in the same impossible soaring curve. Then he showed me how words can be used in the same way. He quoted a verse by Alfred de Musset which is still fresh in my mind – no need to check here:

J'ai perdu ma force et ma vie
Et mes amis et ma gaiété
J'ai perdu jusqu'à la fierté
Qui faisait croire à mon génie. . .

The words building up, rising in crescendo to 'jusqu'à', to the point at which 'life' gives way to 'genius'. Since then, I have sought for 'keystone' words in the poetry of which I read great quantities nowadays, and found them in those which seem to me to reach the greatest perfection, especially in the Shakespearean sonnets.

So René Gimpel taught me that the artist's role is to discover the secret harmonies of life and to interpret them in his own medium. Now I am forced to wonder if he was right. The few years which have passed since then have forced me – and I suppose everyone else – to view art, indeed the world itself, in a new perspective. André Breton has said: 'Art must be convulsive, or cease to exist.' When I look at Picasso's *Guernica* or Germaine Richier's tortured sculptures, I try to remember if René Gimpel ever spoke of them, and what he said. He was curious about everything. I think he meditated so deeply on the works he bought and sold and those he studied in museums or in the artist's studio, that he discovered essential harmonies where none seemed to exist. I often consult him in my mind and try to imagine how he would have interpreted works which to me are so disconcerting.

I remember he told me about Chirico's 'prophetic' portrait of Apollinaire. The painting is distorted in Chirico's manner and shows a hole in the forehead – and that hole is in the exact place where a bullet crashed into Apollinaire's skull on 17 March 1916 – nearly five years later.

In his studio in the rue d'Assas, Ossip Zadkine looks like a mythological tortoise straying in the petrified forest of his sculptures.* Pipe in mouth, followed by Arthur the cat and four staggeringly beautiful American girls, he wanders, talking over his shoulder. At the table, Valentine Prax pours Russian tea for two Japanese admirers, an old friend from Holland, another just arrived from Rome, and myself. We sip, gazing into the depths of this stone forest, where Zadkine's neat, slim figure appears and disappears between the stone trees.

Zadkine must be the last great talker. He talks with only a slight Russian accent, words flowing, not torrentially, but in a light, clear stream that bounds gracefully from subject to subject: about a plant which grows only in the South-West where he has his home, about cooking, poetry, his project for a statue in Caracas, the best way to catch trout in the Lot. No one interrupts. Zadkine uses words in the same way he uses clay, stone or bronze, to build up a world all his own, yet which seems somehow familiar. Perhaps this is how Mallarmé talked during those Tuesdays in the rue de Rome, leaning against the white porcelain stove, a plaid shawl folded over his shoulders. . . Or Oliver St John Gogarty in the sleazy Dublin cafés, back in the days of James Joyce. People whose talk can still be heard across the years.

* Ossip Zadkine (1890-1967), Russian sculptor, lived in Paris from 1909. Famous for his monument to the destruction of Rotterdam, *Destroyed City.*

Ossip Zadkine

Zadkine tells us about the great wooden Christ he had been working on for twenty years and finished a few weeks ago. A lorry brought it to Calus and the men of the village carried it into the church where he had been married, and set it up there. It was fair-day, he tells us, and all the farmers and the peasants, the buyers and the sellers crowded in and filed past, and the whole scene might have been taking place in the eleventh century. The country people, he says, understood the statue at once. They found it beautiful and only regretted it had no colour. 'It's fine now,' one old lady had said, 'but it will be finer still when it's been painted.'

Remembering:

Another encounter with Zadkine, in the Café Select. He suggests dinner. Fried eggs and chips, beer, an ice to top it off. He sits opposite me and I watch his relaxed, attentive tortoise-face. He likes to impress and to charm, but this is not a neurotic need for him as it is with X and so many others. It is his pleasure, his pastime, a sort of hobby in between bouts of work. He has a hundred sculptures at sea, he tells me, on the way home from Tokyo. 'Such wrapping and unwrapping. . .' he sighs, sorry for himself, but his hands make loving movements, as if following contours beneath paper and string. I laugh and tell him he will enjoy himself with his paper-bound statues and he laughs too and admits: 'I enjoy all the gestures of life.' If he had time, he says, he would like to make his own tools, as he did in London when he was sixteen and apprenticed to a cabinet-maker. An old artisan-workman taught him then how to make helves and handles, and he loved to feel them grow in his hands.

Helves and handles lead to the story of his youth. . . His father sent him from Smolensk to a dreary boarding-school in Scotland. He ran away, came to London, apprenticed himself and learned how to file and polish letters carved in wood, and to do other small jobs. One day the same old workman gave him a ten-centimetre cube of wood and told him, 'If you want to get regular work, you should make something of your own to show what you can do – a rose, for instance.' So he worked at his rose every night, while the months passed, and when he had finished each petal was transparent, so that it seemed like a real flower. He took it to a school of art and showed it to the sculpture-master, who accepted him as a pupil.

While he tells his story, I imagine the petal-shaped wood, see it growing thinner and thinner under the little, sharp knife, till he holds it up to the window and sees the light shining through it. 'Each time I go to London,' he says, 'I search the curio shops and market-stalls in the hope of finding it. I don't really believe in it any more, but I still go on looking.'

English writers were flooding into Paris, being admired, fêted, translated. Most of them wore a somewhat bewildered, or apprehensive look, like men floundering in strange seas. Eluard and Aragon, when they went to London, enjoyed this cross-Channel hero-worship. They told stories of their adventure, read their poems to us, and didn't seem to mind at all that only a few people in the audience really understood what they were saying. In spite of wartime privations – surely worse than any we endured in London – they seemed less exhausted by champagne and late nights than the English visitors I interviewed for *Paru*.

Thus I had my second meeting with T. S. Eliot. He was tired and languid after several days spent in the glare of Gallic publicity. I found him in one of those big, impersonal flats used for the reception of distinguished visitors. His big body crushed into a too-small armchair, wide, shapely hands folded over a light-grey waistcoat, immobile in this attitude because a red-bearded young artist was sketching his portrait; alternately reticent and talkative, relieved perhaps to be speaking English. But this time I could feel anguish beneath the calm reserve and perfect manners.

In the café on the street corner, I noted scraps of our conversation, scribbling fast to fix them on paper before they faded from memory. I had asked him a journalist's question, but it was also the one to which I most needed to find an answer. I had asked him whether there would be any place for individual creation in this new world beginning to take shape around us. At about fifty, Eliot had devoted most of his life to the lucid observation of human existence and its absurdities, and had transposed his observations into poetry so as to give them meaning. He must have asked himself this question many times and since then a good many other people have put it to him.

The interview published a few weeks later is there to remind me what he said.

> I am sure there will always be creative activity. That is part of the very nature of mankind. But it is impossible to foresee what form it will take or how far it will conform to what we now call poetry. The raw material of all art is the world within which it takes shape and no one can foresee today in what direction the world will develop. Since we belong to the present day, our own poetry is already pre-determined. We can develop it but not change it. . . perhaps the poetry of the future will take some form so different that we should not even recognize it as poetry. There has always been evolution of this kind. Ask youself what Chaucer would have thought of Shakespeare, Shakespeare of Milton, Milton of Wordsworth, and so on.

Eliot seemed to me a very cerebral person, one of those writers who can stand apart from their work, weigh it up and keep it under control. Graham Greene, when he came to Paris a little later, seemed by contrast immature, still in the process of evolution. Another large man, with a round face which should be ruddy but was greyish when I met him from too much literary lionising. Something suggestive of a sailor – a look strangely common to Englishmen abroad and which they shed on returning to their native shores. In the lounge of the sophisticated Hotel Montelambert, where journalists lurk behind every potted palm, he looked out of place and even slightly flustered. He avoided 'I's' and 'me's', preferring the 'one' which seems to make it easier for him to speak about himself. He was nonchalant about his novels. 'One writes first to amuse oneself, then to amuse other people.' I asked: 'Isn't there some sort of common leitmotiv?' and he said: 'I suppose there is. It's that phrase: "God so loved the world", you remember? I write about a world so difficult to love that only God can do it.'

My little book on François Villon is almost finished. I started it in London when the Reading Room of the British Museum had just reopened, and now I work on it in the *Bibliothèque Nationale*.

Nearly every morning, I bicycle down to the place du Palais Royal. Then I wheel my bicycle through the Gardens, thinking a bit about Colette, writing away in her apartment above the arcades – then I push it up the steps of the passage Beaujolais and out into the rue de Richelieu.

Once inside the reading-room, there's a sort of cozy familiarity about the place, the same smell of ancient dust, the special sort that clings to books. The people too seem familiar. They sit there, isolated each in the small pool of light from his or her individual lamp, and something about their faces suggests that, however little they may resemble each other, they belong to the same tribe. There are one or two I am almost sure I have seen in London: an Indian with a pile of folios beside him, studying with an expression of almost religious intensity; a haggard woman with plaits of greying hair wound round her head. Isn't she the musicologist I talked to in the cafeteria, almost the first day after the books had been brought back from their wartime hide-out?

Here, I go through the catalogues down in the basement and fill in my slips for all the books I can find about fifteenth-century France. I have been reading the *Journal d'un Bourgeois de Paris* ('They do say,' he writes in 1431, the year of Villon's birth, 'that a witch had been burned in Rouen.' So much for Joan of Arc) and other contemporary, anonymous accounts of the period. I try to imagine the Paris they tell of: the great famine, wolves snatching children from their doorsteps in Montmartre, then the Plague and people dying in such numbers that 'they were buried in layers, thirty or forty at a time, barely dusted over with earth.' What a strange epoch it was. It becomes more real to me each day as I resurrect it in little patches, discover streets where I walk nearly every day, and the students' quarters, and the Sorbonne on the same site, and Notre-Dame, all aflutter with doves on Whit Sunday.

I begin to find, underlying the remoteness of the décor, curious remniscences of our own time. The Middle Ages and feudal society crumbling away and the new civilization which was to become the modern world, still unformed. A time of vacuum, unsubstantial and full of contradictions. Aren't we heading for just that? Or perhaps already involved in it? Suppose one could gaze into history just as a clairvoyant gazes into her crystal ball? Would it tell us about the future? Villon grew up in a destabilized world, full of misery and violence and changing values and immense intellectual curiosity. It produced poets like Villon, and aesthetes like Charles d'Orléans, and realists like Louis XI, and monsters like Gilles de Rais – the drama of that moment during Gilles' trial when the procurer rises, trembling, to veil the crucifix so that the face of Christ should not be sullied by the recital of such crimes.

So I observe the hangers-on of Saint-Germain-des-Prés, scruffy as Villon and René de Montigny and Colin le Cayeux must have been, and wonder whether among them. . .

V

Dear X. . . You say you cannot understand why I want to 'go rushing off to Palestine'. Yes, I know it's distant and dangerous and the last place any sensible person would wish to go to at this moment. So since you inquire, I will take another look at my motives, which are not entirely clear even to myself.

The practical part you know already – newspaper and publisher combining to pay expenses, then just standard rates for articles. This means a rather furtive, poor-relation entry into the world of journalism, but at least it's a beginning. Perhaps I shall want to go further; perhaps not.

The rest is harder to explain. I think it started when I read Arthur Koestler's *Thieves in the Night*. It suggested a country where people are making a fresh start, a country about to be born. During my first months in this post-war Paris, everything seemed fresh and exciting, as if I had been plunged into some kind of joyous revolution. There were new books, new pictures, a new way of dressing, new words being used, a burgeoning of life after the dreary years of war. Then I began to feel more and more that all this was happening on the surface – a sort of veneer which allows us to persuade ourselves that our lives have been profoundly renewed. Now the first excitement of return has worn off, I understand that we are still sunk in the past, our feet imprisoned in its swamp, and we drag and drag and can neither be free of it nor relive it as it used to be. We're caught between nostalgia for the past and disillusionment about the present.

So I want to explore a new country and a new way of living, and maybe explore myself at the same time. Isn't that what travel is really about, discovering foreign parts of the world and of oneself?

I'm not really afraid of a little more violence. I saw so much

of it as a child that I was, so to speak, already in training when
the war came. Childhood memories are full of it – hounds
tearing foxes to pieces, my mother triumphantly displaying
the bleeding corpse of a pheasant or a rabbit. Such things occasionally reappear in my nightmares and are far more terrifying
than anything which happens in the daytime. Aren't the things
of the imagination always better or worse than reality?

So I've booked a third-class passage for Haifa. Most of the
other passengers, I'm told, will be Jewish emigrants. (The
agent told me this and paused, giving me time to object, which
I think he felt I ought to do.) The journey takes ten days, with
a stop-over at Alexandria for refuelling. This seems a long time
for a fairly short voyage and suggests a ship due for retirement
after wartime service. We sail in a couple of weeks.

There are records of what followed: newspaper-clippings;
notebooks where yellowing pages are covered with an improvised shorthand, struggling to keep up with voluble Jews,
nervous Arabs, tetchy British – all giving their opinions about
what has happened or was about to happen. They were all
wrong, of course. Nothing ever turned out as they expected.

I find it hard now to realize I was temporarily involved in
the events to which such notes refer. They belong to a domain
in which I have sometimes wandered, but as a tourist, never
as a resident. None of them really concerned me. My own
Palestine was forming itself, concurrently, out of precisely
those things which are of no interest to historians. Bits and
pieces of it reappear in a scrappily-kept diary, mostly dateless,
so that I must sometimes wonder in perplexity: when did it
happen?

This question has, in fact, little importance. The journey
out and the months that followed remain enamelled on memory, sharp-outlined and bright-coloured. Time has not blotted
out people and places, but it has done its work on them in a
different way. It has simply made them irrelevant. Nothing
which happened during those months, nor the people concerned, exist now in any recognizable form. Even the good

ship *La Providence*, once the pride of the Messageries Maritimes, was on her last voyage, already destined – as I had suspected – for the scrap-heap. As for her passengers, they had simply expunged their past, at least so far as that could be done by a conscious effort of the mind, and were now waiting for some kind of future to take shape. Meanwhile, they belonged to an intermediate species which the laws of Evolution – not Darwin's kind, but the accelerated sort which take place in man's inner being – have since rendered extinct. If Nahum the soldier, Josef the teacher, Mosché-from-France, or little Frieda who believed she would find a family awaiting her – if any of these are alive today, they now call themselves Israelis; they have a country of their own, homes, everyday jobs or retirement pensions. When I knew them, they were merely the raw material out of which they would later recreate themselves.

The Europe these people left behind them belongs to the history books. It had left its traces on them – in the tatooed numbers, for instance, which had replaced their names in Auschwitz or Bergen-Belsen. As for the new State for which they were bound, it was still waiting at that time to be born. The passage between the two chapters remains an indeterminate zone which has little interest for chroniclers of the period.

All this has become clear now that events have arranged themselves in a more or less comprehensible pattern, but at that time, they were like a stirred-up jigsaw puzzle before the pieces have been fitted together. Eighteen months later, the country to which I was going would have ceased to exist; people and certain landscapes would have become unrecognizable. At that time, of course, I suspected nothing of such mutations. I had then no more idea of what the future would bring than had the hundred and fifty legal or illegal immigrants crowded with me in the ship's grimy depths, together with some priests and nuns, an eccentric English spinster bound for Cyprus (where she intended to start a new life, having heard good reports of its climate), and a Lebanese woman, returning from Bresil with her baby.

So here I am, lying in my bunk, dizzy with seasickness and *hora*. Whenever I stop being sick, I crawl up to the third-class deck, where the Jewish passengers seize my hands and whirl me into their round. The old ship creaks and shivers and ploughs its way through the Mediterranean. '*Shalom, shalom, shalom aleikum,*' sing the emigrants, their faces desperate with hope and fear, singing louder and louder to the accompaniment of Nahum's frenzied accordion. When they are not dancing, they are down in the dining-room, teaching themselves Hebrew. They crouch over their exercise books at the long trestle tables, tracing the cuneiform signs with their forefingers, mouthing difficult sentences. The few Orthodox ones sway back and forth as they recite to themselves, just as they used to do in the Talmudic schools. They have learned the Holy Books by heart, but not the words they are going to need out there: 'How much?', 'spare parts', 'soil erosion'.

On the fourth day, the Straits of Messina. Sun breaking at last through the clouds. All the passengers up on deck; bejewelled Egyptians, French bankers, Jewish Agency officials, all from the first class; missionaries and suburban English from the second; we, the proletariat, are viewed with suspicion. We may be carrying fleas or infectious diseases.

Scylla and Charybdis tower above us. An erudite Franciscan quotes the *Iliad*. We slide out into the open sea and watch, silent, while Europe disappears gradually from the horizon.

Sudden melodrama. An old Jewess, never yet seen to open her lips, flings up her arms in the primitive, age-old gesture of tragedy and begins to scream to the skies with all the force of her lungs. She screams in Yiddish, standing there at the deck-rails, shaking her fists at the faint, blue mass of disappearing land, screaming as if at some deadly enemy of her own.

'She says: *Cursed be thou, O Europe! Thou who hast slain my husband, my daughters! May my eyes never behold thee again! May the soil that covers the bodies of my children become arid and never bear again! May even the grass disappear from thy surface! Cursed be thou, O Europe and all those*

78

who inhabit thee!'

Mosche repeats the words slowly, dreamily, like an incantation. Other passengers edge away, shocked, perhaps a little disgusted. But the eyes of the Jews glow. They have never troubled to speak to this ugly, silent old woman, but now she is suddenly one of them, the same instincts, all one family.

It lasted only a few minutes. Down on our own deck, the younger people are resentful. They have been taken by surprise. 'All this biblical nonsense,' someone mutters. Yiddish curses are something which belongs to a rejected past.

Nearing Alexandria now. Thick, warm darkness, enormous stars, shining out of an indigo sky. Frantic activity among my companions. Their nerves tingling with apprehension as we approach the first shores of the Levant. We link arms, dance madly: Russian, Hungarian folk-dances, then more *hora*. *'Shalom, shalom, shalom aleikum. . .'*

Two days later, waking very early in the morning, I knew we must be lying off the port of Haifa. The ship motionless and silent; cabin walls no longer vibrating to the throbbing of engines. Clambering over my cabin-mate's eighteen hat-boxes, I scrambled up to the top bunk to peer out of the port-hole. We were not in the harbour, but anchored now in a sea of palest turquoise sparkling with silver sequins. Out of the sea rose Mount Carmel, an alabaster mountain, flecked over with silver-green olive trees, topped by the great white monastery, changed to pale gold in the early sunlight. Behind the mountain lay the 'land flowing with milk and honey' once promised to the Children of Israel.

The emigrants already up on deck, leaning over the railings, eyes strained towards that shimmering, opalescent mountain. The Promised Land would prove a false promise for many of them. Some would be accepted, some rejected. British battleships lay all around us and every now and then the whirr of a low-flying plane reminded us that these were British territorial waters and the Mandate was still in force.

A motor-boat flying the Union Jack came chugging alongside and a stout immigration officer clambered aboard, followed by policemen and a Jewish interpreter. We queued in the saloon, waiting for judgement.

Shrill protestations in a dozen languages, tears, panic, relief, despair; sweat rolling down the interpreter's face as he listened, translated, relayed questions and long, rambling replies, never quite to the point; identity papers scrutinized for forged stamps and false names. And at last, after long hours, the final separation of the sheep from the goats. Landing barges for some; for others, an internment camp in Cyprus. The longest wait of all for me, sitting apart, unclassifiable and thus a nuisance. The previous day British women and children had been evacuated by government order. It looked for a time as if I should be sent on to Beirut, but in the end I scrambled on to the last barge.

Haifa bathed in crude white sunlight. Its distant beauty disappeared, resolved itself into a slumland, jagged with the screams of Arab and Jewish dock-hands and the wailing of beggars with deformed limbs and glaucoma-white eyes. Pyramids of oranges, stacked head-high on the pavement; unenclosed cemeteries with graveyards huddling at the street's edge; further into the town, flimsy government buildings, surrounded by triple fences of barbed-wire and guarded by policemen wearing high astrakan bonnets. Streets blocked by strolling, gossiping crowds which parted reluctantly to leave a passage for our jeep. They backed away slowly, never taking their eyes from us. The Arab stare was blank and indifferent, a defence-wall, hiding whatever was going on behind it; the Jewish stare was full of sardonic amusement and seemed to say: 'You just wait. . .'

Jerusalem was many places at once, always contradicting itself, sometimes drab and grimy, sometimes bursting into brilliant colours and clanging sounds. First, the suburbs with their dingy Arab houses, then the modern and equally dingy Jewish quarter. The New City busy and shabby, much like any provincial town in pre-war England except for its Hebrew signs and the ceaseless honking of traffic. In the big cafés – the Vienna or the Europe – people sat endlessly over milky coffee and chocolate cakes, discussing the price of citrus fruit or absorbed in newspapers printed in unrecognizable tongues. In the farthest corners, hard-eyed young men and women conferred in whispers: when I approached, they fell silent at once. I was suspect, probably a spy, a member of the hated race which stood between the Children of Israel and their promised land.

Beyond the Jewish quarter, a street lined with shabby Arab shops brought me to the Jaffa Gate, leading into the Old City. I recognized the Gate at once. The shepherd camping with his flock of lean sheep in the shadow of the wall; the veiled women squatting beside piles of oranges as big as grapefruit; a pedlar proffering a tray of sticky sweetmeats; a blind beggar holding out a cupped hand; tiny donkeys – just ears and matchstick legs visible beneath enormous loads – all these had the special familiarity of childhood memories. Searching deep into my mind I discovered a coloured lithograph surmounting a biblical text. It is fixed with a drawing-pin to a cream-washed wall. Where? Searching again, I situate this wall in the parlour of a cottage in my home village. Nothing to tell who lives in it or why I am there. There is just that bright scene, the exact scene I am watching now, but immobilized, frozen into silence. Here it all is – shepherd, sheep, pedlar, donkeys – and beyond the gate, there are the same deep, dark shadows. And there I was, and here I am now, staring into those shadows, and now I am just about to crash through them and discover what lies beyond.

I take just a few steps and the flat, printed darkness beyond the Gate bursts into sound. Short, guttural, make-way cries, strident music played to an unknown rhythm, follow me through alleys half-closed from the sky. Light and shadow alternate here; I might be walking beneath the ocean in some drowned city.

Each street is a different souk. In the meat souk, there are horrid, dangling corpses and crimson, grinning heads of unidentifiable animals. In the sweet souk the stalls are piled with violently coloured mixtures of honey, rice and coconut, all speckled over with buzzing flies. There is the pretty fruit souk, and the souk of the haberdashers with shoddy European suits, tinselled marriage robes, shawls and head-dresses of checked cotton. . .

Priests are everywhere. Brown robes, green robes, pointed black bonnets, round white turbans, hair caught up in frizzy buns at the back of the head; sometimes a woman – a tall, stout bundle under shapeless cotton veiling. All just as I expected to see it, a proper prolongation of the coloured print above a text which brought some forgotten message. But I had not imagined, did not expect, the soldiers pushing their way through the crowd, cartridge belts strapped across their chests, striding, provocative, thrusting their way with grim, strained faces. Waiting to kill, waiting for something that is going to happen, waiting with fierce, expectant faces.

JOURNAL
Lorna Lindsey is a friend of Nancy's – an elderly American journalist, tall and thin, a great beak of a nose, faded red hair. She comes from a rich, solid Presbyterian family in Boston, and she has gone Jewish in the whole-hearted way people do when they adopt foreign causes. For her, the Jews are a heroic, martyred people. In the plump business-men studying share prices in the Vienna Café, she sees the defenders of Massada who died by their own hands rather than submit to slavery. She would like to see them reign in a great Jewish Empire extending over all Palestine and Transjordan. The terrorists of the Irgun are her heroes. She has furtive meetings with their leader, Menachem Begin, a deserter from General Anders' Polish Army. He is in hiding now, with a price on his head. I had a brief glimpse of him – a skinny young man with hard, angry eyes, who clamped thin lips and turned away from me without a word.

Because of Lorna, I live in the Pension Waldes, in the New City – out of bounds in principle for the British. It is a sad place, though cozy in its own way, dimly lit and full of drooping green plants which never get enough sunlight. The clients are little, mild old people who creep about, frightened and wishing they were somewhere else.

Wasn't it André Malraux who said: 'There may be such a thing as a just war, but there has never been a guiltless Army'? The British soldiers here are a new race. Boredom and fear have made them brutal. They march, sullen-faced through the streets, or dash, revolver at the ready, into shadowy doorways. In Ben Yehuda Street, one of them leapt at me, gun pointed an inch from my chest. He would have liked to shoot me, there and then; he wanted to kill, simply because he could no longer bear his life in this land where enemies jump out of the dark, attack, and disappear again. He would have liked me to be a Jewess breaking curfew, then he could have shouted and sworn and rushed me at gun-point to the interrogation centre. I could see all this in his simple, desperate face. As it was, he stammered, ashamed at his own violence, wanting now to confide and explain: 'What are we doing here? You tell me that, Miss.' Then: 'We wouldn't mind a proper war. It's this stabbing in the back gets you down.'

More soldiers emerged from doorways. Searching for arms, for illegal immigrants. A sergeant with a grey moustache inspected my papers all over again, disapproving. This is suddenly a danger area. Only yesterday it was a peaceful street, people going quietly about their business; tomorrow, it will be quiet again and some other street will be full of angry, frightened soldiers using their rifle-butts on doors that open too slowly to their challenge. 'There was a land-mine on the Ramallah Road this morning,' said the sergeant. 'Two of their mates killed.' He sighed: 'This lot were kids in the war. Evacuees maybe, or fathers away in the Army and mothers in the factories. No proper disciple.'

These boys are themselves Displaced Persons, like the Jews

Soldiers searching civilians in Jerusalem, 1947

from Central Europe, waiting in D.P. camps to learn what is to be done with them.

And the harsh, white sunlight, and the khamsin blowing up from the desert, jangling all our nerves.

The Pension Waldes in Hayakon Street has become too dangerous, the Jews too hostile. I have been forced to move to the Hotel Yasmina, known as the Press Ghetto and run by a nonchalent, multi-lingual Arab called Mr Fouad. A tough, square girl called Clare Hollingsworth and I are the only women. The men are mostly Americans, but there are a couple of agency boys from London and a few Arabs (they all say they were educated at Oxford and this may be true) appear from time to time to take a hand in night-long games of poker.

Correspondants go out in their jeeps by day and I wander in the streets, constantly being stopped and interrogated by Jews or Arabs, in or out of uniform. Most evenings we gather in the bar, feeling cloistered and claustrophobic and singing a sort of dirge, which changes and gathers new couplets according to inspiration. At present it goes:

The Stern gang say Shalom
Then they kill you with a bomb.
The Arabs draw their knives,
We're in terror of our lives.
We don't want to get this story,
It's getting much too gory. . .

The Jewish Agency boys are tough, pushy young men who believe in the limitless power of propaganda. Their files are full of statistics; their big cars whirl correspondents to distant corners of the country, accompanied by poker-faced guides who can produce relevant facts like conjurors plucking bright-coloured ribbons from an empty top-hat.

Motoring along the track through the Negev desert to visit a kibbutz near Beersheba, the city of Abraham. A roof of heat pressing down on our heads. Wind stirring up whirls of sand which creeps under finger-nails and eyelids, grates through hair into the scalp. Not a soul to be seen. Only here and there the black tents of a nomad encampment with a tethered camel cropping at spiky rock-bush or occasional cactus.

From afar, the settlement looks like a green pocket-handker-shief tossed down on the sand. Thirty young Jews have created a fish-farm here, an act of bravado, a way of saying: 'There is nothing we can't do.' Pipes crawl like worms over the sand; electric coolers whirr in the desert silence. Fish slither in their tanks, graded according to size. The faces of the settlers are like old earthernware pots, cracked by the sun. They are brusque and unwelcoming, muttering in Hebrew, pretending not to understand my questions. They move in a heavy, mechanical way, as if all their vitality is concentrated in the sheer animal courage needed for just being here.

The Rev. Mr Jones – scooped up like myself by the Jewish Agency, but for less reason – stares disconsolately into the fish tank. 'I don't get it,' he murmurs. He has been sent from the States to report on the situation of the Protestant churches in Palestine, and he resents this uncomfortable and unnecessary excursion. 'Maybe God wants me to be here,' he says, 'but I'd like to know why.'

The sudden Eastern night fell just as we were nearing Jerusalem. The wail of distant sirens moaned through the last grey patches of twilight. Roads, barricaded with stacked kerosine tins. Papers examined; car searched. Another curfew on; orders to hurry back to the security zone. Our chauffeur and guide sitting tight-lipped and stiff-backed. Probably spare-time members of the Hagana, Irgun or Stern Gang.

British soldiers and Arab workmen digging among the ruins of the Goldsmith Club, directed by worried young officers. Stretcher-bearers, bored bcause there is no longer anything for them to do. A YMCA van serving tea to the rescue-squad. Driving slowly past, in spite of shouts: 'No hanging about here!' 'Get a move on!'

A sudden moment of recall. . . myself serving tea to the rescue-squad burrowing into the ruins of the Thames' side wharfs. The misty grey night of an English summer. And the blazing river hurtling past my door towards Hammersmith Bridge.

The Rev. Mr Jones is perturbed by our desert outing. He confides to me: 'Twenty-seven young men and five girls. I can't help worrying about those young people.'

How did I come to know Reuben? Like Aron Cordova, whose connection with him I never understood, he had no place in the stories about contested frontiers, reforestation or bomb outrages which I sent back to France. Nor can I find any mention of our meeting in my own personal notes. Certain phrases he let fall suggested he was a Jew of the Orthodox rite, but he had neither beard nor side-curls and wore only a small velvet cap perched on his frizzy black hair. Sometimes I thought he must be a spy of some kind; once or twice he referred briefly to some arcane or mystical system of thought. I met him occasionally in the corridors of the Jewish Agency, apparently going nowhere in particular. Gershon, the public relations officer, told me: 'Don't waste your time with him. He's of no importance to anyone.'

If Reuben was so insistent that I visit Aron Cordova, perhaps it was precisely because Aron, like himself, was of no importance and would thus obviously count for nothing in the future state.

We followed mazy streets in the Old City and came presently to the Wailing Wall. A lot of men were praying there, foreheads pressed hard against the wall, as if in an agony of supplication. Scraps of paper stuffed every crack and crevice, centuries of mouldering petitions, begging for love, or riches, or health, for all the most urgent needs of mankind. A group of passing children belonged to an enclosed, mysterious world. Pallid and elongated like little asparagus shoots – miniscule rabbis, dressed in black double-breasted gabardines, knee-breeches, long black stockings tied with string above the knees, flat black hats. They walked sedately, their lips moving in some unending prayer spun into their brains. I said to Reuben: 'They look as if they have never seen the sun.' And he replied: 'They have no need of the sun. The sun is inside their hearts.' Impossible to tell whether he is stating a belief or being ironic.

A few descendants of Spanish Jews, the first to return here after the Diaspora, live in tiny houses hollowed in the honey-coloured city-walls near David's Gate. Aron Cordova is a *sofer*, a copyist, who copies the Holy Books of the Bible on to long rolls of parchment to be preserved in the synagogues. 'Come in. Come in,' says his fat little wife, smiling in the doorway. 'A few minutes, if you please, then he will speak to you.'

Aron Cordova sits in the deep shadows at the back of the tunnelled room. Flickering light from an oil-lamp at his side reveals him in profile, bent low over his work, his long eyelashes trembling just above the paper so that they seem to follow the slow movements of his hand. A black beard; a flat hat pushed back from his forehead so that it frames his head like a black halo; by his right hand, a second pen and inkwell and a bowl of water. Sometimes he pauses in his writing, plunges his hand into the water, takes the second pen, inscribes a single word, pausing with moving lips between each movement of the hand.

At first he pays no attention to us. His wife serves coffee, soundlessly. Presently he rises and glides towards us like a long, thin shadow. He speaks softly, using the archaic Castilian dialect preserved by this community.

Reuben translates:

'The people who come from Europe today are strangers to us. They do not come as we came, to pray at the temples of our ancestors and await the coming of the Messiah. They bring with them all the sins of the West. They no longer abide by the laws of our religion. They have come to establish themselves in Palestine by violence and to create a political State in our holy land. In their ignorance, they do not even know that all violence is forbidden us and only the coming of the Messiah can bind us together once more as a nation.'

He sighs, eyes straying to the bowl of purifying water:

'We have prayed for centuries: *If I forget thee, O Jerusalem may my right hand wither away.* The true Jerusalem must remain in our hearts until the Coming. These people know nothing of the Jerusalem for which we pray.'

He turns and glides back to his work without another word. We have ceased to exist.

On the way back, Reuben slips eel-like through the crowds and slips in the same subtle, supple way from too-direct questions. Whatever he thinks of Aron Cordova and that other Jerusalem whose very existence is perhaps unsuspected by the Jewish Agency, he is not prepared to tell me. He does consent though, over coffee at the Europa, to tell me the story of Aron's son: 'You will promise,' he says, 'not to tell this to the newspapers. It happened a long time ago, but it should not be

88

spoken of. It is better not to speak.'

He can just remember Mendl Cordova. 'Like the other boys of the community,' he says; so Mendl must have been a pale, black-clad, prayer-murmuring child, like those we had seen passing with downcast eyes by the Wailing Wall. 'A promising student,' says Reuben. 'When he was fifteen, he knew the Talmud by heart and he had begun to study the Cabbalist writings, of which the new Jews have not even heard. He came to know a group of boys who were preparing to join a collective settlement in the region of Hebron. Their families were orthodox Sephardic Jews like his own, but they had come from Europe and their orthodoxy was more liberal, less strict. They believed they could reconcile the old traditions with a communal way of life and Zionist ideals.

'He was tempted. He read manuals of agriculture and Zionist pamphlets and he attended Zionist meetings in secret. At last he told his father what he had been doing and begged to be allowed to join one of the training camps. Aron Cordova refused, of course.'

'And he obeyed?'

'Of course. Disobedience was impossible for such a boy. He obeyed his father and swore never to see his friends again.'

'And after that?'

Reuben makes a gesture which means: there was only one thing he could do.

'He stayed at home and took up his studies again.'

'And now?'

'They say he had always had some sort of nervous trouble. In the New City, they would say: neurotic. He hanged himself in the kitchen a few weeks later. Aron Cordova never speaks of him but he is very bitter against the Zionists.'

'What do you feel about it yourself?'

Reuben laughs, taps a finger against his bi-focal glasses: 'You see these? I have double vision.'

This land is possessed by a fever of creation. It is creating itself. Nothing is wasted; everything must be of use. Rocks are cracked open, soil thrust into the crevices, conifers planted; human wrecks are smuggled in from Europe, fed, trained for roles they have never imagined. What happens to people, or things, which simply cannot be used? I have not yet discovered the answer.

Here, in the kibbutz of Ein Gev, I am at the heart of this frantic activity. I watch, listen, try to understand. Sometimes I feel as much a stranger here as I did in the house hollowed in the rock by David's Gate; sometimes I envy these people because they are totally involved in the realization of a dream.

Only I am not sure they are all dreaming of the same country.

The Sea of Galilee – calm, smooth, luminous, dotted with fishing-boats, exactly as I have always imagined it. The fishermen may be Jews or Arabs – impossible to tell, since they all wear the same head-dress. They fish mostly at night and the lake is starred then with points of light from the lanterns fastened at their bows. Sometimes they sing a little; sometimes they call to each other – in Hebrew or Arabic, I suppose, but it might just as well be the Aramaic of two thousand years ago. These sounds drift up to the guest-house at the water's edge; sometimes they are drowned by the roaring of bull-frogs stirred to a sudden frenzy of mating in the rushes.

Early in the morning, I watch the fishermen from the kibbutz dragging in their boats, heaving their nets, tipping the leaping, struggling fish into crates for shipment across the lake to Tiberias.

Everything in the settlement is modern, efficient, created for maximum profit and no nonsense. Everything has been carefully, logically planned: living-quarters, children's quarters, shower-blocks, laundry, library, watch-tower; then the farm and the stockade; then the lemon and orange and grapefruit groves, then the banana plantation. Beyond these are foothills, enamelled all over just now with bright little flowers which will last only a few days, because spring sunshine here has the roasting heat of midsummer. The Romans left so many shards and coins in this area that one needs only to scratch the earth to uncover a bit of treasure. I found a splinter of engraved pottery before I was called crossly back. No one knows exactly where the Syrian frontier passes so the Arab guards do a profitable sideline in kidnapping wanderers and demanding enormous ransoms. Two members of the settlement were 'arrested' in this way a few weeks ago and spent ten days in a Damascus prison before they could be bought back.

A few of the kibbutznik are tough, mannerless young *sabra*, born in Palestine and feeling the world belongs to them. Most, though, have been brought in from the Displaced Persons' camps in Germany, or from Zionist training-camps in their own countries. They were shop-keepers, furriers, teachers, musicians, students – anything, in fact, except agricultural workers. Here, they work the earth, and work at the same time at their own transformation. They are like alchemists crouching over their crucibles, or scientists raising a new strain of virus in their test-tubes. Only here, the material they work on is themselves. They remind me of old Father Rzewuski's reminiscences of a Dominical novitiate, back in the days when monks took the hard way to salvation: putting off the old self, overstepping the natural limits of mind and body, losing the individual self in the community. 'The new generation,' he said, 'has not the physical or psychological stamina for enduring the regime we once knew.' Here, the settlers just endure.

Kalman, for instance. I met him in the grapefruit plantation. He was working with such clumsy, unco-ordinated energy that he overturned a basket of fruit and exploded into curses. Sweat poured over his spectacles; mauve shadows hollowed round young cheeks. 'Take a rest,' I suggested but he growled, 'I'm not here to rest.' Later, I saw him in the refectory, listlessly eating *leben*, eyes glued to the pages of a Hebrew text-book. He confided to me that he had no gift for languages. 'It is *essential* for us to speak Hebrew,' he said, so fiercely that he seemed to be daring me to contradict him. 'Essential!'

Kalman is seventeen years old, Hungarian, here for a year on trial. After that his case will be discussed by the whole community and a vote taken.

'Where shall I go if they refuse me?' he asks, not expecting a reply. 'I have no family, no home, no country. If all goes well, Ein Gev will be my home and my family, but it is hard for me. I have many failings and they are watching me all the time.'

One of his eyelids twitches as he speaks. He talks in a low, monotonous voice and seems to be speaking to himself rather than to me.

He says: 'I think my work is up to standard. No one can say I don't do my share and more. But there are other things. Last night, for instance, I could not sleep in the dormitory because of Malachi's snoring. I became impatient and shouted at him – not in a comradely way, you understand, but losing my temper. That's the sort of thing that counts against one here.'

He broods, weighed down by scruples.

'This Hebrew too. . . I can't get my tongue round the language. It looks very bad for me.'

Zdenek says: 'Come to our place this evening. There'll be people. We'll be talking English.'

He and Eva live in the married quarters, in a room which is hardly more than a closet constructed of flimsy pitch-pine. Impressionist prints pinned on the walls,; a shelf with books in Czech and Hebrew. They joke about their kettle, which they heat on a small paraffin stove – an innovation which is considered rather daring and anti-social. No committee meeting this evening, so Josef, the *mukdar*, responsible for public relations, is here with his pretty Austrian wife; and Mosché, the Arab specialist; and a fair-haired young German who smiles but does not speak. A few others appear, drink a cup of Eva's tea, say a few words in Hebrew, then hurry away.

These people are exhausted, drained of energy by heat and ten hours of hard manual labour. Sometimes their eyelids

Early kibbutz near Galilee

droop; they are almost asleep; but they jerk themselves awake and begin talking again with hardly a pause. They will go on talking far into the night, long after I have left them and dropped asleep to the sound of dipping oars and the croak of mating bull-frogs. These men and women have acquired thick muscles and slow, peasant movements, but the habit of intellectual speculation goes too deep to be unlearned. They talk when they should be sleeping, they try to squeeze philosophical meanings out of a life designed to be as simple and austere as that of any other farm labourers. They look tired and ill but these hair-splitting discussions are more necessary for them than sleep.

Josef is subtle and perspicacious, a quiet, gentle man whose youth was spent in prison under Dolfuss, then in a camp under Seyss-Inquart. He has no resentment. He cares only for the kibbutz, for its efficiency, for its spiritual unity. He would be kind to Kalman if he had the time, but no one here has time to be kind. He has explained to me: 'A single dishonest or quarrelsome member can be enough to ruin a whole kibbutz.

We live in a way which makes it absolutely necessary for each of us to be able to rely completely on the others.'

He has guessed my thoughts now and he says.: 'We are a hopeless lot. We shall never lose the old habits of mental speculation and hair-splitting arguments. You will never understand this. The English and Arabs are unspeculative people who despise useless discussion. That is why they can generally understand each other. You will understand our children more easily. They are little *sabra*, born here, belonging to this country. It is they who will carry it forward.'

The children live in their own community, cared for by nurses and educators. They join their parents for an hour or so when the working day is finished. They are stocky and muscular; their faces shine with health and their eyes are clear, unshadowed.

I ride out with Josef and Mosché to visit old Sheikh Muhammad at Nequeb.

The narrow track, fringed with scrub, skirts the lake for a couple of miles and ends at a high stockade of sun-baked, yellow-brown mud. Inside the gates, a dozen or so huts scattered around a wide mud-floored yard. Hens pecking busily at nothing in particular; a tethered camel, reposing on doubled forelegs, thoughtfully chewing.

Now children come tumbling from every doorway – pot-bellies, cropped heads, miniature abeyahs or striped cotton pants reaching down to their ankles. They stare, sucking their thumbs. Someone runs to the Sheikh's house; a throaty murmur spreads from behind the mud walls. . . 'Yehud! Jews!' A dust-black Negro wearing a rag of white turban begins to blow like mad on a charcoal fire in the middle of the courtyard. And Sheikh Muhammad's tall son, Hassan, comes out to welcome us to his father's house.

Sheikh Muhammad must be about seventy. So tall that he towers above us, slim and solid like a pillar in his mustard-coloured abeyah and flowing red and white head-dress. A narrow

94

face with high, curved nose and bright black eyes. He touches his breast and forehead: 'Salaam aleikum.'

The house seems quite large once one is inside, the floor and walls covered with fine Damascus rugs; no furniture except a couple of mattresses stacked against the wall. Beside them, a tattered Koran and a small oil lamp. A few cushions to serve as seats. Nothing else.

Ceremonious greetings. Enquiries about each other's health. Other men drift in – the Sheikh's house is open to all – salute us gravely, then squat silently on the floor. The hangings at the far end of the room move, flutter. . . subdued giggling and a scrabbling sound like mice playing in a cupboard, as the women of the house jostle for a view of the strangers.

Hassan is as tall as his father, slim and supple as a reed. He has a reckless, princely look, like the actor I saw playing Shakespeare's Prince Hal at the Old Vic. A Negro brings him a brass pot full of glowing charcoal and he begins to make tea, serving us himself with the ritual serving-words. He begins with Josef, but his father says something and they both burst out laughing as he snatches the cup back and offers it to me. Mosché translates: 'He says he has heard that in Europe it is the women who are served first. Therefore he is serving you first, though to him it seems very strange.'

This joke continues throughout the visit as we are served alternately with stickily sweet tea and bitter coffee. Each time Hassan presents me with a cup his mouth begins to twitch and he bursts out laughing, while his father claps his hands and calls on Allah to witness how well he understands European ways.

Sheikh Muhammad takes a lively interest in a great number of disconnected events. He keeps himself informed through occasional newspapers fetched from Tiberias, to be read aloud in the courtyard and commented, line by line, during the following days. Visitors come too, bringing the gossip of the souks of Jerusalem, Damascus, Amman. From such sources the Sheikh culls his very decided views on world affairs. He believes firmly that we are on the eve of another great war, which will be won by whoever first makes use of a terrible new weapon called the atom bomb. He has only the vaguest idea, however, of who is likely to fight whom (or perhaps he is too polite to suggest that the Jews may be involved). All these commotions, in his view, take place in a vague region he calls 'the West', where no great prophet has ever been born, where people are obsessed with the desire for power and have ceased to believe in God.

'God protects the poor and humble,' he tells us, 'but the great desire too much power and He always punishes them.' There has been a terrible earthquake, he tells us. He thinks it was in Turkey, where people are notoriously godless.

The Negro coffee-grinder comes in and begins pounding the coffee in a huge wooden bowl, using his pestle to make a sort of rhythmic music – three heavy blows on the piled beans, three quick, light taps on the side of the bowl. Through the open door, I watch the sun setting in a riot of red and orange over the Sea of Galilee. Hassan, huddling his cloak around him, turns to me and enquires for the sixth time: 'Kif halek? – How is your health?'

Time has no more importance. To sit here, to drink tiny cups of black coffee, to enquire ritually after each other's health and to speak of God, is perhaps as good a way of passing the hours as any other. To have complete moral security, to be certain of one's proper place in life's confused pattern; no need to hurry, no desires or regrets. But Sheikh Muhammad chooses this moment to explain to us the benefits his people have gained through contact with the Jewish settlers:

'Before you came,' he says, 'we used to sit all day gossiping and drinking coffee. Now you have shown us how to be as busy and industrious as you are, so we work and till the earth and are becoming prosperous.'

He turns on Josef great dark eyes, luminous with sincerity. The flicker of a grin passes over Josef's face. Hassan raises pious hands and says: 'Hamdul'Illah, praise be to God.'

Jerusalem was a breeding-ground for hatreds and suspicions.

96

Too much history, too much tradition, every word and action mysteriously overweighted, as if it was more important than it appeared to be because of some unexplained relationship with other, long-past words and actions.

So I have come to Tel Aviv and here is a city so new that it seems to be racing and panting to keep up with itself. Enormous buildings covered with coloured stucco are hardly finished before they begin to deteriorate, then to drft from shabbiness to decrepitude. Today's smart quarter is tomorrow's slum, but nobody cares because another smart quarter will have sprung up in the meantime.

Tel Aviv pulsates with such vigorous life that I find even its vulgarity endearing. Streets are jammed with madly honking lorries, bicycles weaving between them with jangling bells. People simply plough their way along the pavements, shoving with elbows and shoulders. Ghita, my guide and interpreter, forces a path for me. Her thick black hair falls like a curtain down to exuberant buttocks straining at tight khaki shorts. 'Lunchtime,' she says briskly, and we halt at a *gazoz* stall for fizzy drinks – bright green for her, bright pink for me – and buns stuffed with sesame seeds.

Advertisement pillars sprout from the pavements, ten foot high, plastered with notices of concerts, plays, variety shows, Chopin, Bernard Shaw, Smetana. 'We have our Hebrew plays,' says Ghita. 'Soon, our writers become famous.' Cafés spill out on to the pavements; each profession has its own. Ghita rushes me into the Yemenite café to see dark-skinned men bargaining over parcels of filigree-work trinkets; into cafés where insurance brokers argue over long columns of figures; into the diamond-cutters' café where Poles and Dutchmen hold their wares cupped close in their hands. I must see everything, admire expensive gowns in the smart dress-shops, notice thinly-stocked shelves in the grocery-stores. 'Bad enemies not allowing supplies,' says Ghita.

Abraham Schlonsky, Palestine's famous Hebrew poet, has his headquarters in the Café Carlton. We found him there, surrounded by his editorial staff – a small, compact man with a mobile face, sensual and alert, twisting at each instant into a new grimace. His lion's mane of grey hair, checked shirt, corduroy trousers, remind me of the poets who used to frequent the Dôme in Paris before the war dispersed them or drove them into bourgeois occupations. When he talks, the breadth of his gestures sends galley-sheets whirling into the air and glasses crashing to the ground.

'You are interested in poetry, in Hebrew life? You will write about us? I should like to talk to you for hours, for days!'

He stops short, breathing heavily. Ghita says: 'Mr Schlonsky speak Russian and Hebrew. English is not easy for him. I interpret.' Schlonsky, snorting like an eager horse, is off again:

'You want to know about our Hebrew poetry? Are you like the other Gentiles who expect us to give them a new Bible? Let me tell you at once that we have no intention of doing so. We look towards the future, not the past.'

He pauses, points an accusing finger:

'You are my friend, but perhaps you are also my enemy. Our enemies would like to refuse us our share of the world, but our friends want to shut us away in heaven. As for us, we are quite ready to share heaven with the Gentiles, but in return we ask them for a little place on earth.'

He beams, enchanted with his own paradox. His disciples applaud:

'Yes! Yes! Shalom, Abraham!'

Schlonsky dreams of a great new culture, at once Hebrew and international. He spreads his arms as he talks; he seems an incarnation of one of those old prophets who foretold the future of the Children of Israel. Only instead of prophesying woe and calamity, he foretells a joyous future of liberty and poetry. The gutteral Hebrew words spill out faster and faster, too fast for Ghita to follow. 'He says: . . . Not the artificial culture of the ghettoes. . . He says: . . . Truly new. . .' She gives up, overwhelmed, but Schlonsky talks on in a flutter of galley-sheets.

Memories exist each in its own climate. Sometimes the memory of an event is less vivid than that of the weather at the time it happened. Memories of the roads leading south from Paris, for instance, have become uncertain, imprecise, but each is encapsulated in the burning heat of that matchless summer of 1940; certain moments in wartime London are inseparable from whirls of mist and heavy raindrops splashing into a steel-grey river; childhood memories bathe even more intensely each in its special atmosphere, one which, for me, hesitates most often between sun and rain, so that colours change at each instant and the whole world is veiled in cloudy uncertainty.

Thus, the events of that Easter in Jerusalem brought thick, black headlines screaming from the front pages of the world's newspapers, but my most vivid memories are of small things, mostly connected with the weather. Remembering Good Friday, for instance, brings a whiff of air still heavy with recent snow. No one, not even Mr Fouad's ancient mother, could remember snow at Easter, but down it had come, covering the city with a thin veil of white. It had melted now but pilgrims shivered in the grey, acid air. They toiled along the Via Dolorosa, some of them on their knees, between a double row of Arab legionaries armed to the teeth. The legionaries had no right to be there at all, but the British had given up. They remained in the Security Zone, waiting for the end of the Mandate.

On Holy Saturday, the sky was still heavy and dark. News of battle reached the Hotel Yasmina at midday and spread buzzing over the wires to editorial offices all over the world. A few correspondents started for Bethlehem by jeep but were blocked on the Hebron Road. They returned lookng pale and shaken. 'I've covered a lot of fighting,' said the grey-haired one, name forgotten, 'but I've never seen such a bloody lot of blood as there was down there.'

On Easter morning, the clouds lifted; a pale, early-morning sky promised later heat. Said, the Sudanese houseboy, brought Easter eggs, painted pink and blue, for breakfast. Fresh-swept

pavements were burnished by the sun. Bells rang sweet and clear from the Old City, telling of resurrection. Even the sentinel at the Jaffa Gate saluted and wished me: Happy Easter!

Patriachal High Mass at the Church of the Holy Sepulchre. . . The voices of the Arab choir-boys, guttural yet still tinny with childhood. From afar, the Latin chant strangely resembled the wailing music of the souks. When I arrived a procession was under way: the Archbishop, preceded by an immense cross of solid silver; purple-clad bishops; robed monks, priests of the Latin and Maronite rites with their embroidered vestments; soldiers of the Highland Light Infantry in tartan breeks; Christian Arabs with flowing head-dresses; nuns of Notre-Dame-de-Sion; some elderly Europeans, faces rapt and devout, their lives centred on the Holy Places, immovable, whatever may happen.

The ceremony is too long, the chanting too loud, like a ballet so well-regulated that the movements have become mechanical. I wait outside. Bright sunshine now and the air quivering and vibrating with the chiming of all the bells of Jerusalem. Ringing out from every church and chapel of the city; a solo ringing from one point, joined by another, then others, the heavy bass bells and the light gay sopranos, the chanting from the church drowned now by their ecstatic carilloning. The tight-packed crowd are in a festive mood, women and children, Christians and Muslims, all quivering to the sound of the bells, ready to dance to them if there was room to move their limbs. . . Only the soldiers of the Liberation Army, come up from Hebron, bigger and fiercer than the Palestinian Arabs, scowl and mutter among themselves, angry at these alien rejoicings.

Now the great silver cross appears, framed in the archway. At the same moment, a crackle of gunfire from the direction of Mea Shereem. the cross wavers, retreats an instant – some kind of argument is going on. Borne boldly forward now, with the Archbishop and his acolytes close behind; the procession begins to spill out into the sunlight, down the steps, out into the narrow streets leading to the site of the Resurrection.

Encased between high walls, suffocating with heat, deafened by chanting, it inches forward like a great, multi-coloured serpent, with the cross at its head and myself, almost smothered, carried along, baking in the walled oven of the street.

More shooting now, coming from the Jaffa crossing. Somewhere ahead the choir sings louder, the singing broken by short, nervous silences. Arabs come running from side-streets, guns in hand, stare for a moment at the spectacle, then disappear as if jerked away on a string. A heavy canon begins firing from somewhere on the ramparts, sending long, booming echoes down the streets.

I am lost. Pushed and jostled by the crowd, I have somehow been diverted from the main procession to become part of another one, apparently heading for the Omar Mosque. A chanting, screaming crowd, pressing after some object covered by a piece of sacking and carried aloft by four soldiers. Someone grips my arm. A growl, a shout: 'Yehuddine!' Papers are examined; a lot of talk in Arabic and suddenly the mood changes, I am a welcome visitor, part of some unexplained carnival. A soldier clears a path for me. I am everyone's friend. 'You lady jornalist? We show you very nice thing. You tell in newspapers. . .' He laughs, showing twin rows of fine white teeth, delighted as a child at the surprise in store for me. A space cleared, the tray set down. A cry of triumph and the sacking whipped away.

Memory stops there. No precise mental picture, because I shut my eyes so quickly that they were not forced to register hair or features. Nothing visual, but my brain told me there was a bloodily severed head resting on a wooden tray. I heard: 'Jew', 'Hebron' then, 'You give ten piastres, please.'*

---

* The Arab Higher Executive was furious about the incident and issued a statement about 'this barbarous image of our people'. I believe the organizers of this profitable business were caught and thrown into prison. Next day, though, I was offered a trayful of fingers taken from Jews killed in the same battle. Two piastres a piece was the price. – C.M.

I have forgotten too how I left the Old City. The main procession had broken up, I think, and the Archbishop was being hustled to safety. A few bells were still ringing and the firing seemed to be coming from everywhere at once.

Bethany was gay with the red and yellow gowns of its women. A last road-block at the edge of the village, and then a feeling of peace among unarmed people going quietly about their business. We spin down the vertiginous mountain road to the soft, green plain, all palms and flowers, and the city of Jericho encircled with the just perceptible traces of the walls, brought tumbling down by Joshua's trumpet-blowing legions.

Down now to the Dead Sea, zigzagging to the lowest point of the earth's surface, the deepest pit of the rift torn through Africa in some gigantic, prehistoric convulson. Chateaubriand once looked down over this valley and believed at first that a great encampment lay below. I had the same impression, but the tents were really conical formations of the khaki-coloured earth. A poisoned landscape which reappears from time to time in my nightmares, becomes a background for horrid happenings which fade when I wake.

At the Allenby Bridge, lorry-loads of skirted warriors from Glubb Pasha's Arab Legion were passing into Palestine in defiance of British Army orders; a long file of taxis bringing refugees from Jerusalem or Haifa was drawn up in front of the customs house; there were British armoured cars from the Air Force station near Amman; cars flying pennants of all the Arab States, bringing politicians and diplomats to consult with King Abdullah in his palace at Shuneh.* The Middle East was preparing to explode in some still unpredictable way.

We manouevred, showed passes, argued. Then we were in Transjordan, on a road which dropped in a precipice on one side and rose on the other in high cliffs with caves, where

---

* Abdullah Ibn Hussein (1882-1951) was made ruler of the British Mandate of Transjordania in 1921, and became king when the Mandate ended in 1946.

nomad families made temporary homes. Suddenly, there were fields of dark-blue lupins, stretching away as far as we could see, as if the sky had turned upside down and come to rest on the earth.

JOURNAL

Amman is more like a tribal village than a capital, nestling around its Roman arena at the bottom of a rocky bowl. Embassies, government offices and barracks are foreign excrescences; they have a flimsy, temporary look, as if waiting to be submerged in the next tidal wave of their own history. The town is crowded with refugees and not a room to be had for love or money. The Spanish Consul in tears because his Ambassador arrives tomorrow, with daughter and three secretaries and has wired for rooms with private bathrooms; the Belgian Minister is sleeping on a sofa in someone's sitting-room; the only other hotel is the El Raschid, not normally frequented by Europeans. But the situation is not normal so here I am, and here too are seven engineers from the Imperial Pipe-Line Company, and a lot of heavily-armed men come to enlist in the Yarmuk and waiting for orders to cross the frontier.

The Hotel El Raschid was designed by a mad Surrealist, or perhaps by a contractor who got bored or went bankrupt half way through the job. Only two storeys are finished and above them is the rough sketch for a third, which remains roofless and windowless, its walls stopping abruptly at irregular levels. The hotel thus occupies a great deal of ground space but has only seven bedrooms. Mine is about the size of a largish cupboard, with a small, high-up window overlooking a lavatory. All the furniture has been moved out, so there is just space for two beds. One is for me; the other is occupied by a smiling, speechless Arab lady.

There are at least fifteen servants here. They seem to exchange jobs or do nothing at all, according to their mood. Sometimes Aisha, the village woman with tatooed cheeks and forehead, brings my breakfast. She sets the tray down on my knees, then, taking up her position at the foot of my bed, legs

103

straddled and stomach thrust well forward, she gives me my daily lesson in Arabic: 'Bara'd,' pointing with a dramatic shiver to where the window ought to be; 'Esh', 'Malah', digging her finger at the bread or spoon. Or it may be the one-eyed child, Ali, who wakes me while Aischa is busy in the kitchen, cutting up slabs of meat for dinner. The meat is not beef or mutton and can only be camel.

This evening, the Arabic-speaking engineer sat with me in a dim corner of the lounge, pretending to read *Al Akhbar*, relaying scraps of conversation. 'Iraquis,' he whispers, then: 'Those are from Damascus. They are asking each other: *How can we hope to win this war when our soldiers drink alcohol and flout the laws of the Prophet like drunken pigs?*' A dark-skinned Moroccan bursts in, a huge revolver strapped to his hip, roaring he has come straight from Marrakesh, ready to leave this very moment to fight for the Liberation of the Holy Land. Three Yugoslavs, sent by Tito to train volunteers. Another group – faces built in a familiar pattern – 'Hush,' says my engineer. 'Don't speak now. Those are Englishmen, deserters from the Palestine Police.' Towards midnight, a lot of singing at the bar. 'Mostly about Jewish blood spurting under their knives,' says the Pipe-Line man.

Sometimes I feel I am watching an uproarious, farcical play whose astute author has dropped hints that violence will soon break out on the stage.

In bed I read T. E. Lawrence on King Abdullah, with Lalla, my room companion, lightly snoring beside me. The feeble light from the ceiling does not bother her nor, apparently, does anything else. She expresses herself with gestures and shy smiles. She wakes early, dresses beneath the bedclothes, dabs khol round her eyes and slips away. Somewhere there must be a husband.

Thirty years have passed since Lawrence finally made up his mind about Abdullah, decided he wouldn't do, couldn't be sufficiently trusted to be set up as Sharif of an united Arab State delivered from the Turks. He coddled imaginary ailments, says Lawrence; he was self-indulgent, insincere, ruled by religious prejudice because he was too lazy to think for himself. Now he is ruling over this small, artificial State and, I am told, using considerable subtlety in keeping his more belligerent subjects in check.

The 'Palace' is really just a long, low bungalow where the King comes down from Suneh twice a week to conduct State business. It is heavily guarded yet curiously accessible, much like Versailles under Louis XIV when anyone 'decently dressed' could walk in and get a sight of the King. I arrived at six am, and a little, grey, wizened man in a tarboosh took me to an office, or study, with plain, ugly mahogany furniture. A number of men wearing European clothes and tarbooshs sat on hard chairs round the walls. Another, a man with fierce black eyebrows and moustaches, was fiddling with papers at a desk. The King sat, rather unnoticably, in an armchair in a corner. He wears a snow-white robe and a round, white turban and is still much as Lawrence described him after their first meeting: 'short, strong, fair-skinned, with a carefully trimmed brown beard masking his smooth, round face and short lips'. The beard is grey now and the eyes, which Lawrence found so merry, have grown heavy pouches and look sad and tired. His manner is so kind, gentle, and indeed paternal, that I felt it would be indecent to ask any question which might embarrass him. Perhaps this is part of what Lawrence described as his 'insect subtlety'.

'Ask me any questions you like,' says the King, beaming gently as he waves me to a seat. He may speak only through an interpreter and there is no such thing to be found, just a thin eager young man who speaks elementary English. Soon I find myself wandering in a meaningless labyrinth, always thinking: this must be the way out, but it only opens into yet another winding passage. Time passes and I realize at last that we are waiting for something. 'Please speak just as you wish,' purrs the King. Does the interpreter really know so little English that no reply is ever quite to the point? Then I remember that H.M. is said to be one of the best poets in the Arabic-speaking world. He smiles; he wants to talk about poetry rather than war. 'I write a little poetry. You have been told this?' I say: 'Colonel Lawrence wrote it of you long ago.' His eyes twinkle, his face lights up in a slow, sly smile: 'Colonel Lawrence believed he spoke very good Arabic. We let him think so, so but it was sometimes hard to understand him and we laughed among ourselves.'

He is eager to talk about Lawrence, perhaps because this enabled him to avoid possibly embarrassing questions. He talks slowly in a low, musical voice, sometimes pausing to laugh gently to himself, his eyes questioning: 'Do you find this a good story?' But the story, as relayed through the interpreter (and I begin now to understand that this man has been deliberately chosen for his incompetence) is so long and intricate, with so many references to people and places of which I know nothing, that it is as incomprehensible as it is no doubt meant to be. I do just grasp that on some occasion during the desert campaign he foxed Lawrence and let him believe he had won some argument about money and men. The long, meaningless story winds on, punctuated with sips of coffee. I begin to think it will go on for ever, when Colonel Broadbent, the British liaison officer, arrives, very cross at having been dragged from his eggs and bacon at this unearthly hour of the morning.

So the King stops telling his story, takes Colonel Broadbent's hand in both of his and gazes up at him with loving, trustful eyes. We all sit down again, more coffee arrives and there is suddenly an interpreter standing at the Colonel's elbow. 'Please ask me any questions you wish,' says the King, smiling at me with the same look of trust and affection.

So I ask him the questions I am supposed to ask. When they are indiscreet, the Colonel gives a little cough and we pass to another subject. The King gives, I suppose, the answers the British wish to hear: He feels himself to be the rightful King of Palestine, but the Jews should have an autonomous State because they have suffered much injustice. . . a lot more, too, but I am drugged with fatigue and doped with coffee and it becomes harder and harder to follow him.

Somewhere during the talk, a brief, disturbing interruption. The door bursts open. A young man enters, unannounced. He wears full Arab dress – a robe of white silk, a silken *kefeyah* held in place with a head-rope of twisted golden threads. He stands for a moment, eyes fixed on the King with a look of the most venomous hatred. He remains silently staring for a moment, then turns and leaves the room without speaking.

Colonel Broadbent tells me this was Talal, the King's son. 'They don't get on,' he says. Surely an understatement.*

Back in my room in the Hotel Yasmina. Not sleeping because some of the correspondents are playing poker, noisily, next door.

Tomorrow I shall drive with Nassib Bulos, my Christian Arab friend, and Sam, out here for *Life* magazine, back to Amman, then round by Deraa to Damascus and up to Beirut. This is the only route not cut off by the fighting.

I lie here, thinking about this country which, in a few weeks' time will have a new name and new frontiers. I think about Tel Aviv, about those uncouth young men with their hairy legs and tight shorts, and the girls with their dark curtains of hair and pistols tucked into their belts; about Ein Gev, and the lean, neurotic young men and women come from Europe and trying to force themselves into a mould where they will never fit; about Schlonsky, gazing now into the future with joyous certainty; and all the other people I have met, each dreaming of a different country which he calls by the same name: Sheikh Muhammad and his son Hassan, who are perhaps keeping watch at this moment, long-barrelled rifles

---

* King Abdullah was assassinated in Jerusalem just three years later. A lot of people in his own country hated him for his tolerant attitude towards the Jews, and it was generally supposed that Prince Talal had some hand in the affair. He was interned shortly after in a mental hospital in Switzerland – C.M.

pointing over the mud stockade, shots cracking over the water, and at each shot a yell: *Allah akhbar!* and the soft, round, sad King in Amman, dreaming of an Arab Empire he knows will never come true.

VI

An unsettled, in-between year now. . . . An inordinate amount of time spent in crossing the channel between Newhaven and Dieppe – always, it seemed, in rough seas. Sometimes it was London, sometimes Paris. Notes and letters are dated from one or the other, or not dated at all. Remembering people and events, I am often unsure to what time and place they belong. So I pick out whatever happens to have been preserved in diaries or folders, or whatever just surfaces on the stream of memory.

A letter to Nicolette Boillot in Rabat:

Here I am, back in London (temporarily or permanently? I still don't know) staying in Inez Holden's cat-ridden flat. The cats are mangy, because they are never let out, and they leave tufts of hair on chairs and carpets. Inez types upstairs; I type downstairs. We drink innumerable cups of tea in her sitting-room and improvise adaptations of Shakespeare, replacing names with those of ourselves and our friends. Thus time passes while I try to make up my mind about my future.

Life here is strangely austere. People cling to wartime habits as if fearing it would be reckless or frivolous to discard them too abruptly. We still have our ration-books, for instance, and we queue meekly for packets of tea and squares of mouse-trap cheese. In fact, we still have a lot of the inconveniences of war without the compensations, such as underground dancing and Bernard Miles's 'Late Joys' which used to enliven our evenings. On Sunday mornings, I join Dylan and John Davenport in the Chelsea pubs, just as I used to do. Dylan still spins his fantasies in that rich, plummy voice which used to rivet us to our wireless-sets, he still gives his imitation of a Welsh

109

revivalist preaching about Daniel in the lion's den ('Did that lion snarl? No. .o. .oo. . Did that lion roar? No. .o. .o. .o'), but his face is pock-marked now with alcohol and he sometimes becomes angry for no apparent reason. Cyril Connolly is glum and glowering; he has refused my Mallarmé article because, he said, he is 'sick of French 'flu' and is orientating *Horizon* towards domestic affairs.

I think we miss all those Freedom Fighters who brought drama into our lives. When the streets were full of them, all got up in their uniforms and medals, one had the impression that London was the centre of the world. Now their various headquarters are abandoned, turned into working-girls' hostels, or offices for theatrical agencies or import-export businesses. There are just the restaurants to remind us of their passage. They serve spicy stews and shish-kebab instead of boiled mutton and cabbage and this has changed the smell of London pavements.

And so much, and such totally unexpected things, have happened to so many people. Yesterday, I passed by the old Czechoslovak Institute. It reminded me of Jan Masaryk, who was big and jolly, not at all a suitable subject for tragedy.* He told me I should come to Prague after the war and he would show me the Hradjin and the Charles Bridge. And now we hear he was thrown out of his window, body left lying on the pavement. . . I suppose because he was Minister for Foreign Affairs and insufficiently docile to the Soviets. Clementis – did you know him? – has been hanged, for reasons which remain obscure.

And the Karolyis: there's a 'For Sale' sign over the Free Hungary Club in Connaught Square. Michael K. was Minister in Paris till quite lately. I lunched at the Legation only a few

---

* Jan Masaryk (1886-1948), foreign minister in the Czech government set up in London in 1940; when the Communists took control in Czechoslovakia in 1948, Masaryk fell from a window in his ministry in circumstances still obscure. He was succeeded by Vladimir Clementis (1902-52), who was forced to resign in 1950 and was later hanged.

months ago and was amused to see the table still set with the gold plates and dishes of the Hapsburg Empire. Catherine gave 'cultural evenings', with everyone in evening dress. I heard Louis MacNiece reading his own poems in that soft Irish voice, and Hedli Anderson half-reciting half-singing ballads about beautiful, dead young heroes.* I thought then that Michael was going to fulfil a destiny which has always been snatched from him at the last moment. But when I called on them last time I passed through Paris, new, grim men had taken over the Legation. There are various rumours. Some say Michael was caught and shot (or hanged) during his last visit to Hungary; others that he escaped and they are both in the South of France, but ruined. . .

Leafing through that old engagement diary, I find 'Stevie' jotted down for various dates.† Stevie Smith was just beginning to impress on London a fringe-personality which isolated her painfully from her surroundings, although she was the most inveterate of party-goers. When did we first meet? I think it must have been back in 1942, in the offices of Mass-Observation. She stood in the doorway, waiting for someone, I suppose, a small, dark, skinny person, gazing sharply around her, taking everything in, yet remaining curiously apart. At first sight, I took her for a schoolgirl, because of the pre-adolescent figure and the navy-blue coat-and-skirt and the sailor hat perched on the back of her head. Then I saw the old-maidish lines marking an unfulfilled face and thought she must be full of sorrow and non-experience.

Later, we became friends. She was touchy and aggressive, a mixture of naïveté and sly wit. I understood that under the jaunty exterior, she was out of step with the world, or like a scale with one note played sharp instead of flat. She was always

* Louis MacNeice (1907-63), poet, then married to the singer Hedli Anderson.
† Stevie Smith (1902-71), poet and novelist.

exhausted, forcing herself to stay erect when she would have liked to lie down.

Once, I made the long, intricate journey to Palmers Green, where she lived with her aunt in a big Victorian house. There was a drawing-room, filled with large, sombre furniture. The aunt she called 'the Lion of Hull' was large and square. She sat in a big armchair from which she seldom seemed to move. She welcomed me kindly and thereafter said nothing at all. Stevie did most of her own housework, which she found conducive to creative writing. I imagined her wandering with brush and pan in the big, unlived-in rooms, gazing inward at the private part of herself where she kept her poems.

We visited a schoolgirl's bedroom with a narrow iron bedstead under a white counterpane. She complained of an aching back after sitting up till one in the morning reading a book for review in the *Spectator*. I asked: Why not read in bed? But she had no bedside lamp and the suggestion that she might install one seemed to startle her. She reflected, weighed up pros and cons, then said: 'Perhaps'. But I could see the idea was altogether too revolutionary for her.

One day, Francis Wyndham took me to tea in Braemar Gardens, where Miss Compton-Burnett* (no one would have dreamed of calling her Ivy) was kinder to me than she apparently was to most other people. Memory reveals her sitting erect, reminding me of one of those plants which wither away on crackly, unbending stalks. Slender, wrinkled fingers, loaded with topaz and amythyst rings in heavy Victorian settings, hair arranged in what looked like a tea-cozy on top of her head, the table laden with sandwiches, cakes, always with potted shrimps, like a glorified nursery tea. Everyone was trying, and failing to make literary conversation. Short exchanges of sentences, then sudden icy silence. Like one of those sadistic

---

* Ivy Compton-Burnett (1884-1969), author of a number of experimental novels, e.g. *Manservant and Maidservant* (1947), which influenced novelists in England and later in France.

characters in her own novels who drive friends and relations to madness or suicide by innuendoes and unsaid cruelties. I recognized the rules of the game. My grandmother had told me: 'Never work a subject to death.' Working it to death meant returning to it after two, or at most three exchanges. Anything further might be classed as 'showing off', which was the worst thing one could possibly do and would soon lead to exclusion from decent society.

I must have attended at least one of those tea-parties in Braemar Gardens before June 1949, for here is a diary entry to remind me that I attended a 'Decade' on 'The Preservation of Literature'. It was held in the lovely Abbaye de Royaumont, near Chantilly, which had now reopened as a Cultural Centre.

JOURNAL

Walking in the forest with Nathalie Sarraute.* Small and thin, strongly jutting features. Large, dark eyes, full of some fear or anxiety she never expresses. Dresses anyhow, not caring.

Her childhood in pre-revolutionary Russia — people and small events, evoked with great precision in her slow voice, rhythmed to the pace of our walk. They stand out, sharp and bright, against a background of wide, frozen river. Then Paris, then a year at Oxford. She gazes into the lush greenery, her rather deep voice becomes light and clear, like that of a young girl: 'I thought I might die of happiness.'

She is like most of the French novelists I meet here – she wants to sweep away the past and start all over again, as if *La Princesse de Clèves* and *Clarissa Harlowe* had never been written. 'The novel is a dead form, I should like to invent a new way of describing how people really live, how they think, go straight down into their minds. . .' She speaks intensely, as if her life depends on this quest. I tell her about Ivy Compton-Burnett who reveals everything about her characters through

* Nathalie Sarraute (b. 1900), pioneer of the *nouveau-roman* in post-war France.

113

dialogue, without description or intervention on the part of the author. Nathalie leaps on her like a cat on a mouse, wants to know more. Already there's a page writing itself in her mind. Already, I think, she is preparing to buy her cross-Channel ticket. Miss Compton-Burnett will probably be pleased. She ordinarily refuses to discuss her own work, but she shows a reluctant curiosity about what she calls 'foreign writers'.

'If any who are of real interest come to London,' she said languidly, 'Tell them I shall be glad to have them at tea.'

Remembering:

Stretched out on the grassy lawn before the Abbey, I lie in bliss. Ancient trees, lush with greenery, are outposts of the forest; on my left, a pearl-grey lake; on my right, spires and cloisters still suggestive of Cistercian peace and gravity. The sun shines gently. There is a distant smell of hay. Birds sing. A coming young novelist reclines beside me, discoursing on the influence of Heidegger on the modern novel. On my other side, a coming young poet is telling me about his love life. They pay no attention to each other, but speak sometimes simultaneously, sometimes in turn. Sometimes I listen for a moment to one or the other but mostly I just breathe in the smells of forest, grass and hay.

A bell clangs. The birds stop singing. All over the lawn, intellectuals rise up, brush the grass from their backs and hurry, clutching their notes, to the vaulted hall of the Abbey. For the next three hours we shall discuss whatever subject is on the agenda. It may be 'The influence of politics on literature'; 'Music and Literature'; 'The Relationship between Poetry and Prose', and on each of these every delegate will have a great many ideas and will express them with the unquenchable fluency of the French intellectual – none of the comfortable 'Well. . . um. . .er. . . I sort of think. . .' in use with English writers forced into public speech. He may have profound and serious things to say, or he may be incoherent and inclined to stray from the point, but he will talk on until

Royaumont

the ten-minute bell on the chairman's desk has rung two or three times. The Italian delegates are even more voluble and go on even longer, using wide gestures to enforce their points.

It doesn't matter anyhow what one says or how one says it. No one really listens. These official debates are a way of fixing the spotlight on oneself, of imprinting one's image on other people's memory of the Congress. The real exchange of ideas happens in the village bistro, where we air our personal obsessions about such things as the effect of listening to a Bach sonata while writing at the same time a critical study of dialogue in the modern novel; or whether Paul Valéry's Monsieur Teste is actually a self-portrait.

JOURNAL

Yesterday evening, exhaustion was beginning to set in and the Kafka charade never really got going. Finally we gave up and played records on the gramophone, then Marcel Arland told us a story he had discovered in the manuscript of a twelfth-century sermon he had discovered in the Bibliothèque Nationale.

(I've forgotten to note anything about Arland, who is our Chairman or President, chosen, I am told, after a tremendous amount of scruples, heart-searchings and plain calumny. It had to be someone blameless from every point of view, and few such people exist today in France. Marcel Arland is as safe a choice as can be made, and tipped for the French Academy. He writes beautiful prose; novels mostly set in inaccessible rural districts and thus keeping well outside politics; author of a novel – L'Ordre – which seemed revolutionary in the 1920s but today is symbolic of a safe, middle-aged France which set standards before the war, yet proclaims itself open to change. As a pillar of Gallimard, he is much courted by young writers in search of a publisher. In appearance he is rotund, with a perfectly round, bright pink face and owl spectacles.

Marcel Arland was also a close friend of André Gide and sometimes one has the illusion that Gide is the real chairman of this Decade. It doesn't matter that he is old and ill, and lives

116

somewhere in Normandy. His spirit still presides here. He is an arbiter, a referee. Arland can put a stop to any awkward question with: 'As André Gide once said to me. . .' This quells even the group of aggressive young novelists who argue as if they are tossing hand-grenades into the assembly. They have all called on Gide at least once and have noted every word he said, ready for use in the memoirs they will write when they become famous.)

So back to last evening: Arland told us his story and it was like a return to childhood – curled up on a hearth-rug or on someone's lap, hoping the story would go on for ever and bedtime never come. . . He told us:

'A monk was reading in his cell, when a bird of bright and beautiful plumage flew through the window and alighted on his bed. When the monk rose and would have taken it in his hands, it slipped from them and disappeared through the window.

'The monk left his cell and, going out into the grounds, found the bird, which seemed to be awaiting him. It flew slowly before him and the monk followed it some way into the woods, where it flew into a tree and there began to sing in such exquisite strains that the man forgot everything in the delight of listening.

'Presently the bird ceased singing and the monk turned to retrace his steps to the abbey. After a moment, it seemed to him that the landscape had altered in certain ways, but his head was full of the song and he paid little attention. When he arrived at the gates, a porter, whose face he did not recognize, barred his passage and refused him entry.

"What does this mean?" asked the monk, "I am Brother Ambroise and I live in this abbey."

"There is no brother of that name here," said the porter.

"Nor do I know you," said the monk angrily. "Where is the porter, Brother Clement?"

"There is no porter of that name," was the reply.

"Bring out the Abbot then. He will tell you I have lived here for many years."

'When the Abbot came, the monk saw he was as strange to him as the porter had been. Nevertheless, he began to explain his case, naming the Abbot he had known, and a number of the monks. The Abbot then said to him:

"I recognize all these names, but they belonged to men who lived in the abbey three hundred years ago."

'The singing of the bird had been so beautiful that the listening monk had been plunged in ravishment for three hundred years, which had passed like a few minutes.'

For the people who heard that old sermon, the singing of the bird must have figured the joy of religious meditation. The monks who lived here, in this abbey until some fifty years ago would surely have recognized the allegory in the same way. Yet today, in this particular time and place, the meaning has changed. We discussed it sleepily, while the gramophone played something by Debussy, and the story was now an allegory about the quality of literary style, which draws the reader in its train, making him forgetful of all but its own perfection.

It would be nice to leave it at that, for the monk and his bird were surely the most fitting conclusion, whatever the interpretation, to ten days given over the imagination and the intellect. However, neat and congruous endings are few and in real life it is the *queue-de-poisson* or the anti-climax which rounds off most of our experiences.

On the last afternoon, we visited the Château de Chantilly, which houses the Condé Museum, with its famous collection of paintings and miniatures. It is closed at present, but we were admitted by special favour of the director.

Everybody was in high form. We were met at the entrance by a guide with a powerful Auvergne accent, but he was quickly submerged by some fifty surging intellectuals, all stimulated by the prospect of spending a couple of hours confronting a rival art. Occasionally the poor man's voice could be heard, trying hard to recite his set piece about the Connétable de Montmorency or the history of the panelling, but it was soon drowned by the loud tones of two or three writers chasing hard after aesthetic parallels.

'The line of this Ingres drawing reminds me of the passage where Proust says. . .'

'One detects in Gericault something of the Balzacian approach to contemporary society. . .'

And so on from room to room from Botticelli to Poussin, from Delacroix to Renoir. The guide had given up hope and listened in silence as Marcel Arland swept his flock towards the miniature Room.

We were examining the portraits of the ducs d'Aumâle when a larger and fiercer guide, bedecked with epaulettes and medals entered, accompanied by our own guide, who wore the grimly happy expression of one who is about to get his own back. Number One clapped his hands to draw our attention then announced in portentous tones that the valuable silk cover of a sofa in one of the rooms had been barbarously damaged.

We followed him to the scene of the crime and contemplated in crushed silence a small tear near the arm. The culprit was then invited to own up.

After a moment's deathly silence poor R. admitted. He had indeed leaned against the sofa in order to get a better view of a Delacroix battle-scene and the silk had split under his hand. He produced a Foreign Office card, mentioned the sales of his latest novel and added that he was prepared to pay for any necessary repairs.

'That is all very fine,' said the guide in effect, 'but a certain Monsieur Marcel Arland, as leader of your party, is responsible for your conduct.'

Marcel Arland is not a patient man, nor used to being treated without deference. Angrily he commenced the recital of his chief works, of the associations of which he is a member, and in general of his claims to fame. The guide listened with a face of granite, waited for him to finish, then remarked woodenly:

'That is all very well, but a sofa is a sofa.'

The Director now arrived on the scene – a peppery old gentleman, who obviously disliked writers as a class, or at least writers who disturbed his holiday. We were treated to a long lecture about our behaviour and to his own views about people who had no respect for art treasures and barbarously defaced ancient monuments. R. – now looking about two feet high – stood apart and forgotten, though still protesting pathetically that he was a person of importance, a distinguished novelist and ready to pay.

'Sir,' said the Director, suddenly aware of his presence, 'you do not appear to comprehend the situation. A sofa is a sofa.'

We trailed out in silence, and until we were well out of the grounds, not a word was said about Proust or even André Gide.

It occurs to me now that this story is just as moral as the one told by Marcel Arland yesterday evening. Everything is relative, it seems, even the importance of literature.

Paris seemed in many ways to resemble the city I had known before the war. Food was back in the shops, buses back on the streets; new literary reviews replaced the old ones; Culture was in full swing. A letter to Walter Strachan, written during a first, long stay, tells of my preoccupations at the time (spring 1948):

> I am deep in the Palestine book which is getting daily more and more like every other travel book that has ever been written. You, who wisely avoid prose, don't come up against the transport difficulty which darkens my literary life. I mean, the awful problem of getting oneself or one's hero from one place to another without those endless 'then I went' and 'he took the broken-down old station bus up to the village.' You know. A travel book is practically all 'then I wents', or else a series of magic-carpet arrivals which leave the reader far behind. I don't know any solution. . .
>
> Next time I see you, I hope I shall be less incoherent than I must have seemed last time. At present I am well and being very mondaine and have two pretty New-Look dresses.

There remain, too, a few letters from Nancy Cunard. In the

first days of return, she had been a bridge between past and present, between war and post-war. She would appear and disappear, always unexpectedly, always absorbed in some lost cause, bubbling with rage or enthusiasm, refusing to recognize any truth which did not fit into a pattern established once and for all in her mind. Then suddenly there would be a letter from Toulouse, where she was involved in some complicated political plot with a community of exiled Spanish Republicans. Then a gap, nobody seemed to know where she was. And now, here is another letter, from Lamothe-Fenelon this time, and she has acquired a house and finds herself faced with the harsh realities of housekeeping ('I am so tired of cooking for self. To hell with eating.'). Nancy wrote as she talked, inconsequentially, sometimes in love with her house, sometimes hating it. A letter, written when she was still in the honeymoon stage (no date, of course, but probably from Summer 1949) has survived removals:

Ah but now I have a house: incredibly small and elementary but I adore it and adore this region and know it and shall know it far better in time. I have no desire for Paris, and thank God this is 9 hours distant, which keeps away the bores and may not impede the few one really does want to see, who knows? But the house has taken too much time already, on account of the state it was (and is) in. No sheets, etc. No lavatory, no water. Superb electric light and divine neighbours who load me with gifts, eatable gifts. I wish I had NEVER seen bloody Normandy. Had I lived down here from the start the whole of my life would have been different and I should not have lost everything.

I wonder who told you where I was? Tzara maybe? The arm – it got alright finally, quite cured, having cost over 20.000 francs in the clinic, damn it. Here I can live as cheaply as a workman, and that's all too costly. Appalling is the situation, is it not? How do you manage in Paris?

The Mouth of the Sword is a very fine title, I think.* Of

* Published by Routledge in 1949.

what is the book? I shall read it with very great interest I know. My darling American friend wrote just now that Palestine is the touchstone (of war-not-war) in the US. I hate the Americans more than ever, and with what cause; there are so hideously many of the wrong sort. Does hating get one anywhere, you may ask? Not-hating doesn't either, and hatred of filth seems just part of one, no?

I had known very few people in Paris before the war, and even fewer writers. Later encounters in London had had a special flavour because bombs, danger and homesickness had somewhat blurred national or individual characteristics. Back on their native soils, exchanges were sharpened by a new aggressivity, a competitive spirit in the matter of recollected sufferings, privations, or heroic resistance. So the international congress of the PEN Club held in Venice in September 1949 was stimulating and occasionally quarrelsome. I sent an account to Walter Strachan.

First I was in Bordighera [. . .] and was just deciding I couldn't manage the PEN at Venice because funds had run out, when I discovered that an Anglo-American company was turning a film nearby: *My Daughter Joy* with Edward G. Robinson, Richard Green, Norah Swinburne and Peggy Cummings. I slipped into it somehow and found myself acting 'stand-in' for Norah S. This is by no means grand and simply consists in being a sort of tailor's dummy moved about in front of the camera till they get the right angle, when the star comes on, fresh as a daisy, and one hobbles exhaustedly away. It was fun though and I got a sight of film life behind the scenes. I was also in a crowd scene as an extra, so when it comes on you may perhaps see me floating around, very much in the background in the ball scene. Anyway I earned enough to get myself to Venice and had a hectic PEN week [. . .] The things that stand out are, first of all, Monteverdi's *Coronation of Poppea* given in the arena at Vicenza. I did wish you could have been there, dear Walter, it was absolutely unique and indeed so perfect that

I feel I shall never want to go to the theatre again. First, there was no curtain and no scenery except intricate and wonderful perspectives of arched and columned streets at the back. Thus there was none of the division between actors and audience we are used to. We simply sat in a half-moon round the stage, then wandered on it between acts and inspected the scenery. Half way through, a very nice little kitten got on to the stage and listened attentively to the music without seeming at all out of place. Singers marvellous; Seneca reminded me of Chaliapin, who I heard as a girl just before he died.

There was also a very grand ball at the Rezzonico Palace. I felt like a dogaressa sweeping down the canals in my ball dress. The PEN women of course were rather plain, but there were the most beautiful Venetians, in such dresses as you never saw. Then of course churches and churches, hundreds of them and indeed far too many beautiful things to be taken in in one week. [. . .]

Nancy was there, looking very nice and staying in her cousin's palazzo, where she gave a delightful cocktail party one afternoon. Day Lewis was there, (Cyril) Connolly, Alex Waugh and Auden (with an atrocious little blond cockney boy-friend in tow, Chester by name, who called him Darling at the top of his voice all the time. Really!).

Another letter, dated September 1949:

I promised news from Venice and here I am, and here too is practically everyone else. People who were mere names to me now have faces and their particular kinds of behaviour. The Italian delegation, for instance, is headed by Ignazio Silone, who has not yet been heard to speak except from a platform. He sits through official lunches and dinners without opening his mouth except to allow the passage of food. Poor Pamela Hansford Johnson, sitting next to him yesterday, was becoming desperate and ended by spilling her wine through sheer nerves. André Chamson, another safe, uncompromised regional novelist, seems to be the chief Frenchman; Jean Follain is here too – a great and still insufficiently-recognized poet, and wonderful company once he is past his third glass. Up to that point, he is apt to be silent and gloomy, then he takes the decisive sip, and off he goes, discoursing on whatever subject absorbs him for the moment. Early this morning, he called for me and took me to San Marco, where Mass was being said at what appeared to be a doll's altar in a side-chapel. Jean stood close up, watching every movement made by the priest, storing every gesture in his mind for future use in poetry, prose or just conversation. We lunched afterwards with Georges Duveau in a restaurant overlooking one of the grubbier canals and he rehearsed the entire ceremony for us, reproducing every movement giving a little sniff at what one was sure must have been the exact point at which the priest did the same.*

As for the English, all the Best People are here – Connelly, Auden, C. P. Snow, Day Lewis, etc. Someone seems to be missing. Virginia Woolf, perhaps? She would have been perfect in this setting.

But what I really want to tell you is this: when the speeches start, I slip away and wander in this extraordinary floating city. Yesterday, I set out early, following small canals and back streets, going just anywhere, exploring churches, peeping into cloisters and courtyards. Somewhere, I came to yet another church, went in, nothing special to be seen. Then a little, grey old man hobbled along the empty aisle and asked me , would I like to see *qualque cosa molta bella*? The church-warden, of course, hoping for a tip. He led me to the sacristy, threw open the door and pointed up to the ceiling: 'Ecco il paradiso terrestre.'

And for a moment I felt I really was looking at the earthly

---

* Ignazio Silone (1900-1978), anti-Fascist Italian novelist, author of *Fontamara* (1930); Pamela Hansford Jonston (1912-81), critic and novelist, wife of the novelist C. P. Snow; Jean Follain (1903-71), poet; Georges Duveau (1903-58), French social historian.

paradise. Sixteenth-century, I suppose – when Venetian merchants were going back and forth to the Far East. The ceiling was all close-massed vegetation – dark leaves, glowing fruits, huge, impossible flowers, bright birds. Not unusual in Venice, but I had the strangest impression of really catching a glimpse of paradise. It lasted only a moment. The sexton was in a hurry to pocket his tip and lock up again.

So I came out into the street and walked for a little while, with the same sight still in my mind's eye. Then I realized I hadn't noticed the name of the church, or that of the street. I turned and took what I thought was the way by which I had come. But I never found my way back. I tried again today. Thought it might have been the Salute, but it wasn't. I have questioned people who live in what must be the right district (*Dove se trova il paradiso terrestre?* My Italian is rudimentary). Then I asked several Italians from the Congress and André Chamson's wife, who knows Venice well. No one has heard of the Earthly Paradise; Michelin is mute; and tomorrow I must take the Geneva Express.

Could I have been dreaming? Tell me what you think. . *

How can one prevent hindsight from creeping into memory? I haven't yet discovered how to do this, and almost always I must ask myself: did I really see it this way? Isn't there something of the present-day me watching in one corner and shifting the scene, just slightly, into a different perspective?

This grandiose reception in Venice, for instance, this welcome infinitely more luxurious than any nation would dream of offering today even to its film stars or pop musicians – this essence of Italian *fa figura* – did I perceive it at the time as a

* I have returned to Venice since then and have tried to rediscover my Earthly Paradise. Nearly thirty years later, an architect who had something to do with the 'Venice in Peril' Fund, identified it as San Sebastiano. The guide books certainly tell of painted ceilings by Veronese, but make no specific mention of my Earthly Paradise – C.M.

sort of farewell? And the two swans, life-size and moulded in foie-gras which flanked the buffet in the palazzo were surely not intended as symbols, but instant association suggested 'swan song'. Hindsight tempts me to think I made the association at the time, but I cannot be sure. Maybe I was just enjoying myself.

So we floated in gondolas, ate the choicest meats Italy could provide, were shown buildings, paintings, sculptures, all miraculously preserved from bombs and advancing armies. Our delegates made speeches, bathed in applause. But the applause was for what they had done, not for what they were going to do. I wonder if they suspected that nothing would ever be quite like this again? That the word 'Culture' would not always have exactly the same meaning? That *Horizon* which had glowed like a beacon during the war years, was creaking towards its end. That back at home there was a hungry generation preparing, not just to tread them down but to trample on them as hard as it could stamp. Even now it was filling fountain-pens, beginning the first chapters of novels about people who for centuries had played secondary or comic roles in English fiction, people who had not been to public schools and whose accents proclaimed their home regions, the grandchildren, in fact, of Mr Kipps. Their names were not yet known and they had not paid subscriptions to the PEN Club.

126

VII

It was through my friend Arnold Mandel that I discovered Isabelle Eberhardt. One day he paid me a visit, bringing with him a rather grimy volume he had discovered on a bookstall on one of the quays by the Seine. It was entitled *Dans l'Ombre chaude de l'Islam* (*In the warm Shade of Islam*) and on the front page there was a photograph of the author, whose name I had never heard. It showed a very young girl with a round, Slavic face, wearing a fez and baggy trousers like those of the Algerian Spahis. Mandel said, 'I think she's someone for you', and left me to make her acquaintance.

I read *Dans l'Ombre chaude de l'Islam* and knew at once that he was right. I searched second-hand bookshops in out-of-the-way streets and at last found a long out-of-print volume of Isabelle's diaries. It had an introduction giving the main facts of her life. A good many of these turned out to be incorrect but it was nearer the truth than the fantasies Isabelle herself wove round her beginnings. Then I burrowed further and turned up a volume of short stories – some of them just unfinished sketches – of desert life. I had all three volumes bound in red leather by a little bookbinder in Montmartre, and here they stand now, close at hand on my book-shelves. I have reread them several times during the intervening years and each time I take them down, even if it is just for a flick of the duster, the pages fade for a moment and give place to the stained and tattered manuscripts I was shown in Algiers: loose pages, partly indecipherable beneath red smears of mud from the bed of the wadi at Ain Sefra. Between the stains, scribbled phrases, lyric ecstasy, upsurges of mysticism; thumb-nail sketches of soldiers, preachers, interfering Europeans; chronicles of long marches through the desert and halts in the bitter night-air of the Sahara. And always this fleeting vision is accompanied by the overpowering smell of cats in Madame Barrucand's flat in Algiers.

So Isabelle Eberhardt moved into my brain and settled down there. She came at the right moment, for the months in the Middle East had held back as much as they had given. Living among Jews, I had been sealed off from contact with Arabs. Sipping coffee with the Sheikh of Nequeb and his son had revealed no more of them than if they had been characters in a play with myself sitting among them instead of watching from the stalls. As for King Abdullah, I had learned more about him from *The Seven Pillars of Wisdom* than anything I had discovered for myself during a couple of hours of uneasy conversation. And the Arabs I had met in Amman and Damascus had been westernized men trained in propaganda and knowing how to slide gracefully away from unprepared subjects. The Islam they showed me had been a political idea, or at most a code of conduct. I had suspected another dimension but had lacked a compass.

It seemed to me that Isabelle – or 'Si Mahmoud' as she later became – might be my guide in this matter. I set out, tentatively at first, to discover her. Prudence, I soon realized, would be essential. Arabs would no longer be quite what they were in her day, nor the House of Islam as romantic a dwelling-place as that which she had raised in her imagination. She had been a mystic, almost a fanatic, a child wandering in a world of intrigues and machinations whose existence she refused to recognize.

Isabelle chose all Islam as her home, but before she came to it, there had been Geneva and the childhood about which she told so many contradictory stories. She may have been laying false trails, or creating her own fantasies, or escaping from plain facts she did not want to face. If I was to follow her into the Sahara, as I was now determined to do, I had to find out as much of the truth as could still be discovered.

JOURNAL
This town [Geneva] was meant to be a mere stepping-stone to

128

Algiers, a place for delving into musty folders and rummaging in city archives for missing clues. But it has proved to be a prudent city, always making sly promises to turn me aside from my original aim. Neither French nor Swiss, it seems reluctant to reveal its true personality. Certainly it remains indifferent to the glass and concrete buildings of international organizations busy about health, food, money and so on. Functionaries of these can be seen hurrying along the lakeside, talking various languages and clutching briefcases, or driving sleek cars along the quai des Bergs. They are intruders who are here, but might just as well be somewhere else.

The old town, however, has a story-book quality which always makes me feel that something is going to happen on the next page. Its flights of steps leading from one level to another suggest a big, rambling country house. It seems cozy rather than calvinistic, but one can never be sure. This *pension de famille* on the Route de Florisand, for instance, is almost too good to be true. Impossible to imagine the demoiselles Rose, Clemence, Françoise and Angéline in any other setting or absorbed in any other activity than ensuring the health and happiness of the various students, secretaries and office workers who lodge with them. A newcomer has hardly unpacked before the sisters have discovered his or her favourite dishes and are hurrying out to buy necessary ingredients. Anyone planning a late night is given a key and told in an urgent whisper: 'Now don't go hungry to bed. Just pop into the kitchen and you'll find something in the fridge to settle you down.' They appear not to notice, or not to understand, the tiptoe comings and goings between bedrooms and they beam innocently on the charming friendship between Mr Paul from Illinois and Herr Sigmund from Cologne. Moreover, they are the souls of discretion and treat our personal tastes as if they were state secrets. 'My little finger tells me you like meringues,' Mademoiselle Françoise whispers to me, 'I've brought some in for supper tonight.' A finger to her lips, a conspiratorial 'Ssssh'.

From this charming base, this pink chintz nest, I followed

the trail of Isabelle Eberhardt. At first there were two notebooks: a 'serious' one for births, deaths, comings and goings (born 1877; died 1904; nationality: Russian; mother: Eberhardt, Nathalie; father: a blank here), and a second one for the various by-ways into which I stray in the course of my search. The trouble is that the two have been constantly mingling and interweaving with each other. Plain facts refuse to remain plain. One thing leads to another and often ends up in a full circle. It is perhaps right that so chaotic an existence should refuse neat classifications.

There was the long tram-ride out to Meyrin. The Villa Neuve stood far back on a wooded common, still isolated and forlorn though a few shiny bungalows have sprouted along the road. The house: dilapidated, with glassed-in verandas, probably once used as hot-houses. A stream running between winter-bare trees and beyond it stretches of rough ground where Trophimovsky, the ex-pope, tried to grow exotic essences. *Shuttered and mute among the weeds, as if plunged in some morbid dream*, Isabelle wrote after a brief return in 1900.

I walked a little way along the road, watching the distant Jura Mountains, on the tops of which a little snow still lingered. Isabelle was thinking of this same road when she wrote: *I was a nomad when, as a little girl, I used to dream and watch the road, the white road that seemed to draw me along it and that wound away, beneath a sun that seemed to me more than naturally brilliant, straight into the delicious unknown...*

The Villa Neuve must have symbolized for Isabelle everyday life, the Reality with which she could never come to terms; and the road leading away from it was first the Unknown, and later became the Absolute, or the face of God.

I've already abandoned the notebooks one and two method. It only creates more confusion.

Then there is the onion-domed Orthodox church. The last remnants of the old Russian colony live in its neighbourhood, as close to it as possible. A few came here at the end of the last century, because their parents had had trouble with the Tsar, or had just been in love with Western culture. Most were refugees from the Revolution.

. . . A stuffy little sitting-room, all plush furniture and portraits of the Imperial family. Four old ladies and an infinitely distinguished-looking old man, gathered round a samovar, exactly like a scene from Chekhov. Their minds wander a little; Russian phrases creep into their talk. They have vague recollections of Nihilists – people to be avoided – who lived in some other part of the town, four or five to a room, it used to be said, always plotting, said to have been involved in some attempt on the Emperor's life. The oldest of the old ladies remembers: 'The police came once and asked my parents a lot of questions. They did not understand the difference between one sort of Russian and another.'

None of them ever met Trophimovsky. 'A friend of Bakunin, one heard,' says the Count. 'A Nihilist like him, a defrocked priest.' They used to hear stories, because the poor woman had once been of their world, wife of a general of the Imperial Army, it was said. They murmur together in Russian, exploring each others' memories, but nothing more can be brought to the surface.*

The city archives have yielded a name: Perez-Moreyra, Jules. A lawyer's clerk. Married in 1888 to de Moerder, Nathalie.

Perez-Moreyra, Marie, whose name followed that of her brother, is still alive. A little wispy old woman on the top floor of an apartment-building in a back street. Memory failing. Searches it slowly for this portion of an evidently unevent-

---

* Isabelle Eberhardt's mother was Nathalie Eberhardt, who was married to General Paul de Moerder and had three children by him. Alexander Trophimovsky, a pope of the Russian Orthodox Church, had come to tutor her son but eloped with the mother and chldren; she had two more by Trophimovsky, one of whom was Isabelle. They eventually settled in Switzerland, where Trophimovsky kept the family in isolation: Nathalie de Moerder, Isabelle's half-sister, escaped into marriage with Jules Perez-Moreyra when Isabelle was eleven years old.

ful past. Ruminates in silence; surprises herself by sudden remembering: 'But you mean. . . Ah, yes, that little Isabelle. . .'. Remembers her well now, and the fuss there had been when her sister fell in love with Jules, because Madame de Moerder's real husband was not that horrid man whose name she can never remember, but someone important in Russia, and they thought themselves too good for Jules, though they were poorer even than him.

The story re-emerges in her mind, slowly, in disconnected fragments. 'I remember how that old man shouted. They all seemed to be afraid of him. He was always taking out law-suits against people in the town, or perhaps it was they who were after him because he never paid his bills. That was how Jules first went there. That little Isabelle, she was much the youngest. At first, I thought she was a boy, because she was quite tall and she had her hair cut short and she was wearing boys' clothes. She was carrying a great sack of earth and when I knew she was a little girl, that didn't seem right.'

Nathalie had told Jules that all the young people had to work for Trophimovsky in his market-garden. 'He used us as his slaves,' she had said.

The *Courrier de Genève* has its archives too – back numbers bound in heavy volumes which emit a haze of dust when opened. Some years ago, it published an article on Isabelle's girlhood in Geneva. I sought out its author and was side-tracked into the world of Professor Weber, President of the International Neurological Association.

Professor Weber has a notebook all to himself, because our talks, which began with Isabelle and often returned to her, opened new perspectives and posed still unsolved – perhaps unsolvable – problems.

Professor Weber is a huge, vigorous old man who takes a passionate interest in an immense variety of people and things. His kindness is such that he cannot bear to fail medical students who come to him from far places to pass their exams. He worries that I am too thin and takes me to smart *patisseries* to fill me with cream cakes. I eat to please him while he tells me about the time when he was a professor in the Faculty of Science in the University of Algiers. Isabelle Eberhardt was already dead, but there was still a lot of talk about her. The French hated her because Europeans – especially women –

Isabelle Eberhardt, aged 19

were meant to live apart from the Arabs and set them a good example from a distance. A few had liked the stories of desert life she published in one of the local papers, but no one forgot the terrible scandal after the attempted murder in the region of El Oued. She had nearly died of her wounds, but the Press was hostile and when the assassin was brought to trial it had often seemed as if she, rather than he, was the accused. Witnesses came to report that she had stirred up trouble among the tribes and the confraternities, that she had been responsible for skirmishes and killings. That was how the French of Algiers saw her – a trouble-maker, probably a spy, leading a dissolute life, not even pretending to respectability.

'Some of them hated her,' says the Professor. He did not like those people, he found them snobbish and boring, so he bought her books and began to discover her, just as I am doing. He marked the same passages as I have done in my copy. She wrote her diary when she was lodging in the rue de la Marine, a horrible little back street, he says, somewhere in the slums of Algiers:

The most difficult of all things, she wrote, *The only difficult thing perhaps, is to enfranchise oneself and – even harder – to live in freedom. Anyone who is in the least free is the enemy of the mob, to be systematically persecuted, tracked down wherever he takes refuge. I am becoming more and more irritated against this life and the people who refuse to allow any exception to exist and who accept their own slavery and try to impose it on others. . .*

Professor Weber was bored by the colonial French and preferred to live among the Arabs. He tells me about his friendship with the Aoussaia tribe, who practice secret rites, heretical for orthodox Muslims. He tells me how they took him to a house in the Casbah and initiated him into some of the secrets. 'I saw them bring the sun down into a copper bowl,' he says. He shakes his heavy lion-head, still puzzled, accepting and refusing both at once. 'I can't believe it was true, but I saw them do it.'

134

Professor Weber took me yesterday to the laboratory where he investigates the mysteries of the brain. A clean, white, quiet place – a long table scrubbed white; a line of cages in which quiet cats doze, heads on folded forepaws; a white mouse, pink-eyed, turns on a wheel; charts pinned on shiny white walls portray the pink lobes and grey filaments with which, it seems, we think and pursue our psychic activities. The Professor, looking something of a stranger in his white coat, is cheerful and matter-of-fact, happy to draw me into his own, particular world. He takes a sleepy cat from its cage, strokes it with large, kind hands, sets it on the table, where it crouches indifferently. A girl in a white coat arrives to immobilize it in some kind of metal framework. Now the Professor takes a thread-thin electrical wire and inserts in with a single, incredibly deft movement into the cat's brain. Instantly, it is transformed into a spitting, raging wild beast, furiously struggling to break free and attack. The girl steadies this furious head between her hands; the Professor touches another point, and in an instant the cat is all purring contentment.

I wonder how Professor Weber reconciles his experiments with the sun he *saw* – he swears it – being forced down into a copper bowl. I have tried to ask him this, but he is not a man for metaphysical speculation. Or perhaps – and on reflection, I think this is nearer the truth – he is perhaps a man who accepts with stoicism whatever must be accepted. Our discussion – if it can be called that – took place in yet another *patisserie* and he evaded it by pressing me to take a chocolate cake.

ALGIERS
The lush scenery of the Tell reminds me of Torquay – too green, too rich, much too far from the Sahara. The town itself is any Mediterranean city – Marseilles with some added folklore of chechias and Muslim women veiled with an inch of muslin. For the Europeans, Muslims mean native servants, shoe-blacks, street-sweepers and the anonymous crowd that invades the rue Michelet at certain hours of the day. The life

of the Casbah and the native quarter down by the port concerns them not at all, but at twilight they become uneasy at the thought of the strangeness and unknown things that lurk three or four trolley-stops to the East. Then they invent contemptuous names – *les bicots, les ratons, les melons* – and exchange over cocktails stories of the misdeeds of their Mauresque cleaning women.

I have made enquiries about Isabelle. A few old people have faint memories of her, and I begin to think the faintness is sometimes intentional. 'We appreciate Miss Eberhardt's writings,' one of them said to me, 'but we prefer not to speak of the person.'

I tried to find the mosque of Djemaa Djedid, where she went for the evening prayer on the day of her arrival in Algiers. I could not find the place, or perhaps I did not recognize it, for guides led me from one mosque to another, from one quarter to another, while I became more and more exhausted and bewildered.

I should like to share a few moments of that mystical fervour, the fervour of the convert for whom Islam was both a home and an escape route:

Entered into the cool dusk she wrote in her diary, *hardly lighted by a few oil lamps. Impression of old Islam, mysterious and calm.*

A long wait near the mihrab. *Then, from far off, behind us, there rose up a clear, high, fresh voice, like a voice in a dream, making the responses to the old Imam standing in the* mihrab *and reciting the* tatiha *in his quavering voice. Then, standing in line, we prayed, between the alternation of two voices, at once intoxicating and solemn; the one in front of us broken, old, but little by little swelling, becoming strong and powerful; and the other, streaming as if from above, out of the depths of the dark mosque, at regular intervals, like a song of triumph and unshakeable faith, radiant. . . announcing the coming victory, the inevitable victory of God and his Prophet.*

I myself have not dared to attend a Muslim service. All the problems of an unfamiliar religion. I know I must take off my shoes – but after. . .? I suspect, anyhow, that foreigners are unwelcome. Perhaps they would send one of those stern-looking turbaned men to order me away.

At the headquarters of the *Gouvernement général* they have given me an open letter to the colonels in charge of the various *Annexes*. So I shall be able to travel freely and stay wherever I choose.

The bus leaves very early in the morning. Tiny shops flare acetylene lamps into the moonlight, their proprietors already astir among bunches of candles and leather sandals. The sun comes up suddenly, swamping the mountains in harsh yellow light. The road winds up to the Hauts Plateaux above invisible valleys, drowned in the sea of clouds. Sometimes the reddish earth is covered with pine groves and low bushes, sometimes it is green with young wheat, though there is never a soul in sight, save an occasional Berber, huddled in a burnous, riding up out of the mist on a skinny mule. At Aumale, snow still powders the grey or ochre-tinted mountains, where flocks of sheep crop at a meagre scrub. The first camels appear. Conical hills, flat-topped as if their summits had been sliced off with a razor blade, jut out of the plain. The structure of the earth changes at this latitude and concave, convex and pyramidic shapes replace the rounded ups and downs of Western landscape.

Bou Saâda among the first dunes that announce the desert – a town of yellow clay rising out of yellow sands, overlooked by the big pink barracks on a table-topped hill. The Grand' Place is carpeted with reclining Arabs. Groups of Oulad Naïl women flit among them, gaudy in many-hued satins, unveiled, heedless of the weight of gold and silver festooned on foreheads, breasts and arms, proudly conscious that they are one and all of holy descent, straight from the Prophet's loins; proudly prostituting themselves in this town and every town of the Sahara for the dowry that will bring them back as wives and mothers to their native mountains. They are there for the wiry Kabyl, the warrior Chaambas, the Negroes of In-Salah and far away in Marrakesh; they are there in Djamaa-el-Fnar for the pleasure of the Schleughs, or the tourists, or anyone who will add a little piece of silver to laden bracelets or head-pieces.

All this comes to me from the officer from the Arab Bureau who joined us at Bou Saâda – the only other European in our bus. He is bound for Touggourt, where there is some kind of political trouble. He has been here nearly ten years, but already Europe seems to him far away and unreal. Next year, a civil Administration will be taking over from the military and the Bureau will be disbanded. He cannot imagine what he will do with his life.

Stony ochre foreground, lilac hills; the scrub has disappeared and the road become a track. Veils of colour drop and lift over the hills; misty blue, lilac-brown, ochre, pinkish-yellow. These changing colours are the only change in this desert land. A single landmark during all these hours – a huddle of stones by the track-side, where the nomads who die in the villages are brought for burial.

Towards evening, the first oasis appears. In the harsh desert, palm-trees spring up; emotion of renewed life, the sense of flowering and growing and the accustomed cycle of birth and death. Behind the clay walls of the first *ksar* there is a glimpse of well-tended palms, of shadowed, sandy earth, of a cluster of huts. Then more desert; then, in the twilight, another oasis, with a half-finished Mission church, where a solitary White Father in Arab dress walks slowly, with the same patient, unquestioning look I have been seeing in the eyes of the Muslims. 'The South has eaten him,' says a green-burnoused Arab, companion of my route, and the two converse unhurriedly while a negro boy brings mint tea, thick and sticky with sugar.

Biskra among its hundred and fifty thousand palms – the last outpost of the tourist, alive with Swiss Germans and shrill

138

with guides, Jewesses swathed in brilliant, filthy rags; a Negro village where black-skinned people flit like shadows between crumbling hovels. The old Caïd, Mustapha ben Yusef, is on my list of people who knew Isabelle, but he will not talk. He has no wish to remember her or anything else of his past. He walks with me among the dunes, tall and silent. I begin to think he has forgotten my presence, but after a time he stops and stands gazing out over the sands, then he says to me: 'All human effort is futile, since each man's destiny was written at the creation of the world.' Then we walk silently back to the town.

Travelling in Arab lorries with passengers huddled on the roof, clinging on as best they can. So far, I have been given a seat. We are in the Southern Territories now, the true Sahara. Scrub-dotted at first, reddish earth, the blue Aurès mountains in the distance, irridescent in the pink dawn-light. The yellow sand, bare of all vegetation, then the white dunes of the Desert of the Souf, sparkling with quartz. Everything is deformed by this emptiness. On the horizon appears a fortressed town rising above an azure lake that reflects its many-storied palaces with their balconies, their moucharabias, their terraces. Now we draw near, and it is merely a sand-cliff and a patch of salt-field, stained with the reflection of the sun.

Bordj Hamreiha – We crawl, stiff and shaken, from the lorry to squat in the thick shade of the walls. The inhabitants emerge, nonchalant, to stare for a moment at the foreigner, then return into the fortress. An old man and a boy return with a goat-skin filled with water and a long-beaked copper jug of tea. A man from Tamanrasset offers me a hard-boiled egg: 'Share, share.' A Negro in a short, kilt-like tunic wanders past, staff in hand. A pearl-coloured bird, heavy-beaked, struts unafraid. My companions lie stretched in the warm sand, propped on bent forearms, staring into the distance.

This is a crossroads of the desert, where the nomads come for water or to haggle for eggs or coffee. Three of them appear now, from nowhere, risen apparently out of the ground. The

139

woman is draped in heavy crimson robes; on her head, a wide turban, intertwined with plaits of her own shining, oiled hair, tresses of black wool and ornaments of gold and silver. Her face has the colour and texture of wood, carved in jutting lines and angles. She is so tall and stands with such noble immobility that she seems a tree hung with crimson rags, growing, leafless and austere, out of the desert sand. The two men are even taller, slender and muscled in their white robes and brown burnous, their razor-lean faces swathed in white muslin. They greet us, 'Salaam aleikum', but to me, since I have no title to the Muslim peace, they say, 'May God open the door to you!' They have come from El Goléa and now they are bound for the Djebel Amour with its summer pasturage. They tell us all this in their quick, grunting language and the Arab sergeant from the Mehari Corps translates for me. He knows their country and begins to talk with them about their flocks and the villages in the far South. But I think about their birth, how they were born at the hazard of a halt under a black tent woven from goats' hair, and how they will die at some unforeseen place where the wind and sand will soon efface their fragile tomb and there will be absolutely no trace left of their passage on earth.

El Oued – the little cupola-shaped houses surrounding the big market-place where the Bedouins come on Thursdays to sell their goats and camels. An hotel run by a fat Greek and frequented by seedy-looking commercial travellers from the Levant. The rich, warm shade of clustered date-palms and the deep quietness, broken only by the creaking of pump-arms as donkeys circle endlessly round the well-heads. And all around, sand gently shining in the sun, pure and white like snow.

Isabelle wrote: *The first vision of El Oued was for me the complete and definitive revelation of the harsh and splendid Souf, with its strange beauty and also its immense sadness.*

This evening, the little town is throbbing with drums. I have arrived just in time for the festival of Sidi Merzoug and the

Negro quarter will dance all night in honour of its saint. They are feasting there now on the ritual sheep in the house of their Sheikh. The Arabs too are invisible since the sunset prayer; the town is at once deserted and expectant. Emerging from the crumbling Jewish quarter, I become conscious of a human presence. Without looking up I know that Yusef and Ahmed are there. There is something miraculous about the ubiquity of this pair. I may take any direction, walk any distance, at some point they are sure to appear and fall silently into step beside me, ready to accompany me wherever I go, giving no explanation and demanding nothing. Ahmed is small and slender, tidily clothed in a European suit, partly covered by a rather grubby nightshirt. Yusef is tall and plump and wears heavy white robes and a complicated turban. He speaks no French but questions me occasionally through the voluble Ahmed on the customs and climate of France. He is always happy and smiling, like a contented sheepdog. We climb the slope, top the crest of the dune, and now the town is out of sight. In the starlight, the sand flows before us, fluid, like a great sea. Far off, a man sings as he fetches water from some distant well – a song all on three notes that tells of the beauty of some unnamed woman, calls blessings on her eyes, her nose, her mouth, her every feature. The fragile, far-off song floats across the white ocean of sand, the only sound in the great silence of the desert.

Presently, as we sit talking, running the chilly sand through our fingers, women pass us on the way back to their village. They walk in single file and at the sight of the men they start, clutch their veils around them and scamper down the slope with little cries of dismay. The sand is like cool silk beneath my bare feet. I could walk for ever, straight ahead, and never come to the end of that great sheet of moonlight.

'What lies out there?'

'The City of Gazelles,' says Ahmed, 'El Menzeha.'

Yusef makes a rapid sign, a magic sign, which he believes I have not seen.

'Where is it?'

'A hundred kilometres away, or perhaps fifty, or maybe three hundred.'

But Ahmed will say no more and begins quickly to talk about Paris, where, he has heard, everyone is rich and a fortune is to be picked up in a few weeks. There is a man who comes each week to El Oued, he says, a very important man who is a friend of the government in France and will give him a paper that will allow him to live there. Yusef gives him half his pay each week and hopes to make the journey at the end of the year.

The summer heat is beginning now. The sun is so high that hardly a shadow falls from the squat little *quoubas* that mark the graves of the saints. A light wind stirs the powdery sand that drifts and dances in a moving mist at the height of my knee. The sun is a burning weight on my shoulders. Suddenly, green plumes wave before my feet, gently stirring in the breeze. I stand at the edge of a garden, a deep funnel scooped in the sand, down to the level of the underlying water-sheet. The tops of the palms are just visible above the surface of the dune and the great pit of the garden is full of shadow and the murmur of water and leaves. I slither down the steep side and find myself in the funnel-shaped hollow, dim, cool and green. The palms form a roof through which the sun throws splashes of light. The ground is tended, manured, divided by clay runnels into neat squares where grow carrots, onions, barley. Everything here is rich and juicy and green. There are two well-heads, constructed of roughly-tied logs. An old man weighs against the jutting arm and draws up from the depth of the well a goat-skin, bloated with water, which empties itself into a clay-lined hollow. From this hollow the water trickles into a channel which branches into innumerable intersecting runnels. Two meagre children run hither and thither stuffing rags at the points of intersection, directing the water in this or that direction, sending it where it will best feed the thirsty vegetables.

The gardeners pay no attention to my presence, but when the labour is finished, the old man straightens himself with a

142

groan of pain and signs to me to approach. He speaks no French but everything has become so simple and direct that we have no need of words. I am a guest in his master's garden. That is enough.

We sit at the root of a great palm-tree. He takes a broken crock of water, a mess of dates wrapped in a cloth. 'Eat in the name of God. *Bis m'Illah.*' The crock passes from mouth to mouth. The water is tepid, brackish, but tastes good in a throat parched by heat and grated by sand. The dates are blackish and gritty – the dates of the poor, the scum of the harvest. As I eat, I watch the sand that trickles slowly down the side of the funnel, slowly devouring the hard-won garden. Day after day, unremittingly, the gardeners must fill their heavy sacks and toil up the slopes to empty the sand back on the dunes. I have seen them often, gasping, spitting, toiling late into the night and when, back in El Oued, I ask the near-naked little boys who beg in the streets where are their fathers, they answer: 'The sand killed his heart.'

The Bachagha Masraeli-abdul-Aziz is a fine old man with long, white moustaches and a pendulous, pock-marked nose. When he drapes his burnous around him or flings it across his shoulder, his gestures are noble, careless, not yet restricted by age. An ex-officer of the French Army, born of an ancient sheikhy family, he is head of all the local *caidate* and serves the French well. When I talk to him about Isabelle, he does not understand at once. For him, she was Si Mahmoud. He says:

'At first, we thought she was a man, but we understood soon that she must be a woman. She spoke Arabic and rode in the fantasias with the best of our horsemen. She was a holy woman. There was much evil talk about her, but here in El Oued, we knew it was not true.'

Sometimes I take tea with him, in company with his new wife. She is a doll moulded in pink and white wax, swathed in pink muslin and flowered silks, her hair looped in shining, jewelled braids over her ears. Though she is tall and fleshy,

A funnel-garden near El Oued

she makes tiny gestures, and she sits immobile, for any length
of time, with a small fixed smile on her face. The Bachagha
plies me with honey cakes and tells me stories of the old days,
of the great sheikhs of the confraternities, of expeditions to
the untamed Hoggar and battles with the faithless Touareg.

Yesterday he spoke of the City of Gazelles, the buried marvel that lies out there, in the heart of the Grand Erg, in the waterless desert which the Bedouins call the Country of Fear. I understood from his manner that this is a subject not lightly to be discussed, and forebore to question too insistently, but this morning his cross-bred secretary brought me a double sheet of foolscap paper. One side of each page is covered with flowing Arabic script; on the other is a careful French translation.

In the year 1919 Sheikh Salem Abdul Ahmed, the Ghedeir of the Chaamba, then 88 years of age, told me that he had heard from the Agha Kelouil Targui of Mogasten in the Ajjeur, that the latter had been told by his father Kelouil that an evil year of drought had obliged them to leave the Ajjeur to seek pasturage for their cattle. They found it at the place called El Ouader (Eastern Erg) between Ramadès and the Souff. They passed the Spring season with the people of the Chaamba and the Troud who pastured there. When the heat began, they heard echoes coming from the dunes, as if of music and drums. The old men of the Chaamba and the Troud said there was a city, built of gold and silver, buried beneath the sand. They knew not where it lay, but the fortune of its people was in wild cattle and gazelles. Their nourishment was of milk and meat. One day Kelouil saw a number of wild cattle and gazelles entering a cavern. After some days he went to Ramadès to seek palm branches to mark the place of the cave. . .

The manuscript breaks off there. If the Bachagha knows more about the adventures of Khalouil, he does not wish to tell it. Perhaps he has in mind the *djinnoun* who guard the Grand Erg.

The track to Touggourt has been buried for years beneath the wind-borne sand. We bump straight across the dunes in Rebuschi's creaking lorry. Rebuschi says 'About ten hours' for the fifty kilometre journey, but when I ask Saïd, the chauffeur, if we shall arrive by nightfall, he smiles vaguely and says, 'If God wills it'. We eat our lunch beside a well, reclining on the shadowless sand. The well is a deep pit lined with concrete. Three Bedouins, says Saïd, died beside it last summer. They could see the water shining in the pit and there was a rope for lowering the bucket, but no bucket, and they had no cup or can, so they died there, at the very edge of the well.

The next halt is at a café at the edge of a small oasis, with a single well and a few clusters of seedy-looking palms. Three men lie on the rush mat in front of a sort of shack. A very old man and a young boy emerge, speak in Arabic to Saïd, then produce from inside the shack a battered chair with a broken bar across the back. Installed in this seat of honour, I observe the preparation of mint tea, a complicated rite involving two pans, the tossing of boiling water from one to the other, the addition of sugar, tea, mint leaves, each action accompanied by some kind of commentary (or can it be a prayer?), the water flung back and forth between the pans so swiftly and dexterously that not a drop falls to the ground.

When the tea is ready at last, Saïd decides the chipped china cup is unworthy of me, has it changed, then: 'You know how world begin?' I admit to being unsure of the facts and he settled down to entertain me with the story.

'When God made the earth, he made sea, fishes swimming, animals, all sorts – dogs and horses and camels and elephants. Then he made men and ladies afterwards. When everything was ready, all nice and finished, God made the pen. And when this pen was ready, he looked at it and thought how good pen he had made. And he said to the pen: "Now write down everything that will happen to the world and all the men and ladies in it, right up to the last day."'

Saïd pauses, making sure of his effect, then adds triumphantly:

'And the pen wrote it all down, everything that will ever happen in the world. It wrote how we come to Touggourt, or perhaps something happens and we do not come. We do not know, but the pen knew it all and wrote it down for God.'

A white-washed cupola rises out of the sand on the outskirts of Touggourt. The *qouba* of Sidi ben Haroun. From the interior rises the muffled sound of a flute and drum. The little courtyard is empty, but inside the *qouba*, through a cloud of churned dust, I can just see three men moving in a shuffling dance round the tomb of the saint. Now a troop of Oulad Naïl arrives in a flutter of silk and a sparkle of jewels to settle like a flock of bright birds in a corner of the courtyard. Then come the laughing, graceful children, then the slow-moving men with their grave gestures. I follow them, crouch with them in the shade of the walls.

No one pays the least attention to me. Perhaps they are too intent on the coming spectacle to realize there is a stranger among them. I ask an elderly man squatting beside me to which confraternity he belongs. He answers in halting French, without turning his head. 'We belong to Sidi. . .', but the name of the saint is too slurred for me to catch.

A youth passes, holding out a bowl for alms. He makes his round, waits for a few minutes, then passes again. Each time, I drop a small coin, but he pauses no longer in front of me than he does before the Oulad Naïl.

Now the marabout himself emerges, tall, lean, black-skinned, with a shaved, conical head from which hangs a single tuft of hair. He has a long, horse like-face with a flattened nose, hollow cheeks and rolling, fanatical eyes. A small blind flautist and a massive Negro drummer follow him out into the courtyard and incite him, standing like storks, each on one foot, with their insistent music. The rhythm, slow and solemn at first, then becomes more and more insistent, with the light, wailing *rhabaiia* following the monotonous beat of the drum. The marabout stalks back and forth in an expectant, jerking prowl. The muscles of his naked torso ripple under his skin as he prepares himself in this prowling, silent concentration, for the coming effort.

147

Suddenly he throws back his head. Three times he howls to the sky, 'Ya Muhammad!' The silent prowl resumes. 'Hamdoul Muhammad!' he cries again and the crowd, with upheld, cupped hands, answers him, 'Hamdoul Muhammad!'

Now he barks out the names of the holy men of Islam: Sidi Tidjani, Sidi Abdul Kader, Sidi Djilani, and other holy wanderers who have passed the sacred flame from generation to generation. I recognize them because Isabelle had much to do with them, begged them often for help and recorded their conversations during halts in the long desert rides.

The marabout's litany is accompanied by some tremendous interior labour. Sweat pours from his forehead, his eyes roll upward till only the blind whites are visible. Now he dances on one foot, a strange hopping dance accompanied by a recital of verses, presumably from the Koran. The crowd repeats the verses with him, but half-heartedly, as if waiting for better things, while the youth takes another collection.

Exasperated now, the marabout snatches up a bunch of dried palm leaves, thrusts them into a fire burning in a corner. The flames flicker over his face; the black skin glows crimson through the screen of fire; a river of sweat streams over chest and shoulders, splashes on to the sand. He thrusts the bunch of flaming palms into the loin-cloth tied at his waist; a pink, swollen tongue hangs from his mouth; he takes great leaps into the air, leaping to the beat of the drum. At last he weakens, falls on one knee with arms outstretched and lolling head. At the same moment, a man seizes hold of a woman crouched beside a cooking-pot on the fire. She is small and light, swathed in green draperies, face and head completely covered with a veil of sacking. The man carries her to the centre of the courtyard, drops her, and she begins to dance, slowly and gracefully at first, then more and more wildly. As she whirls, arms outstretched, the veil drops from her head and she is revealed as a withered old woman. Suddenly she totters, spins round and drops in a faint. Her husband lifts her – she is light as a feather – tosses her aside, and the marabout rises to leap again into the dance.

148

'Ya Muhammad! Muhammad is God's prophet! Allah alone is great!' murmur the Oulad Naïl and the bracelets clatter on their wrists as they move their hands in the eternal gesture of supplication.

Ouargla is a biggish garrison town constructed at the whim of some strong-minded colonel in the neo-Sudanase style, all points and spikes. I lodge in the guest-house, a square hut of *toub* with a washroom jutting out on to the sand. At seven o'clock each morning, I wake to see a very large Negro standing over my bed, radiantly smiling as he holds out a bowl of black, syrupy coffee. After that, I look after myself, buying dates and flat *pika* in the market-place and glasses of mint tea from the café. This spare diet is supplemented by copious dinners in the homes of the little group of French officers. Their wives are glad to see a new face. Apart from short spells of duty in the dispensary run by the colonel's wife, they have

Near Ouargla

149

nothing much to do. There is just bridge and gossip and sand creeping into everything.

The native village is built of *toub* and straggles out around and beyond a market-place surrounded by arched colonnades. All around, there is an immense palmery divided into individual gardens by a labyrinth of clay walls and cool, sand lanes. The Ouargli are Berbers crossed with Negro – a blackish, smiling, indolent people, owning nothing, draped in rags transparent with age, feeding on a handful of dates, a crust, or perhaps nothing at all.

Friday night: the blind muezzin has groped his way up the minaret to call the people to prayer. (He must be blind, Colonel Hays tells me, for the sake of his soul, because of the women on the terraces, who must not be seen, and whom he must not see. There is no lack of blind men in this glaucoma-ridden land.) Now his wailing cry spreads over the town. People hurry from all directions to the chief mosque, not stopping to speak to each other, walking quickly and silently, faces absorbed yet alert. Soon they are swallowed by the mosque and now the chanting flows like a river from the open door, meets and mingles with the prayer streaming from other mosques; the whole town vibrates now with prayer.

And on Friday night the garrison receives its wages. As the first stars shine out into the ink-blue sky, acetylene lamps flare up in the reserved quarter. The Oulad Naïl are waiting in their silks and and satins, golden stars on their foreheads, the golden hand of Fatma at their breasts, their arms stiff with the gold and silver of their bracelets. They lean against the posts of their open doors, beneath the crossed rams' horns, dreamily smiling, their eyes awake and greedy, and the soldiers arrive all together, charging down the lane, singing, wildly laughing, to seize them by the waist, bend them backwards in their lean arms, fasten their lips upon the painted mouths. The women break away with little cries of simulated fear, make little dashes for undesired freedom, flitting between light and shade. The soldiers enter into the game, though their faces are wracked

150

with the long days of abstinence, and the lane seethes with this erotic mime of capture and escape. But at the corner, a young Negro stands a little apart from a girl, his two hands holding her waist. They stand there, tense, gazing into each other's eyes, and the two immobile bodies shiver suddenly with love.

Captain Dubordeaux commands the camel-corps. Sometimes I see him ride out on his racing *mehari*, followed by his *goum*, their cloaks making moving splashes of scarlet against the ochre sand. They visit the villages of the Annexe, to show themselves, to demonstrate that the French are here, in control. The Captain has his own informers, who will signal by a gesture or a whisper that there is an agent from the North, come to preach independence and recruit men to work in secret.

The Captain is a man of the desert, one of those old hands of the Arab Bureau who have lived so long in the Sahara that they have become closer to the Arabs than to the French. He dresses in immaculate khaki uniform, but he goes barefoot, because he can no longer support the constraint of shoes. He dreams of crossing the Grand Erg Oriental from Ouargla to Ramadès – a thing which has never yet been done, though several men have lost their lives in an attempt. 'It could be done,' he says. 'It will all depend on thorough preparation. One party must leave from Ouargla, planting well-signalled water-butts along their route; another will have started out from Ramadès doing the same thing. They would meet here,' his finger jabs at the wide empty space on the ordnance map. 'After that I would start out again with my *goum*.' First he must find a sponsor for the expedition, and there is the problem of his men. They believe the Erg to be guarded by the *djinnoun*. 'They are brave men', he says, 'not afraid of death but strange things happen out there. Sometimes they panic and then it is hard to stop them turning their camels and riding break-neck for home.'

Tomorrow he will take me as far out into the Erg as we can go in a day, first in his jeep, then on foot.

151

The Bedouins call this 'the Country of Fear'. We have left the oasis far behind and before us the desert rolls away, unbroken, to distant Tripolitania. On and on, over the rise and dip of the shifting dunes. The skeleton of a camel lies couched on its side, head thrown back in a final gasp for life. The air is full of the sound of drums and pipe-music: impossible to tell from whence it comes; it rises out of the sand, from the hollows of the dunes, sometimes to right, sometimes to left, and sometimes it seems to hover in the air at the height of our heads, so there is the illusion of an immaterial flute played by invisible lips. 'The wind in the hollows,' says the Captain, but all those years of desert life have untaught him many things, and if I pressed him he would tell me more of the *djinnoun* and the siren music that lures men to their death.

A mirage forms and fades in our path – clear blue pools that dissolve into blue smoke drifting up into the sky. Somewhere out there lies the City of Gazelles.

The Captain knows the story well. Its people, he says, lived among their orchards, in houses of silver and gold, as if in an earthly paradise. But they gave themselves up to debauch and Allah in his anger buried the fabulous city beneath the sand, sparing only the few just men and women who dwelt there. A Bedouin of El Oued, he says, was lost in this part of the desert and almost dying of thirst, when he saw a woman dressed all in white, seated on the ground, caressing a gazelle that stood at her knee. At his appearance she rose and disappeared into a cave. The man followed her through a tunnel and came at last to the abandoned city. All day he wandered in the silent streets or in the orchards where grew a profusion of exquisite and unknown fruits. Then he returned by the tunnel and out into the dunes. He found his way back to El Oued as easily as if some invisible guide had led him by the hand.

This Bedouin had been careful to mark the way by dropping white pebbles as he went. When he came again to El Oued, he told his friends of his adventure and three of them set out with him to follow the track and discover the wonders of the buried city. But the *djinnoun* had displaced the pebbles and they were led astray, far onto the waterless Erg, and no one ever saw them again.

The Captain finishes his story. At a little distance before us shimmers a great lake, full of the swimming shadows of palm-trees. A slight ripple stirs the water; the low wail of a flute drifts from the farther shores. Three steps. . . the music is stilled and the softly mounting smoke is all that remains to mark the place where the lake has shone. Now we must return across the sands where no track is to be seen save those of our own feet. In certain sheltered hollows, say the Captain, those tracks may remain for years.

Somewhere out there, in the vast triangle formed between El Oued, Ouargla and far-off Ramadès, lies El Menzeha, the buried city, where all the gazelles of the desert return to die.

Isabelle never managed to reach Ouargla. She dreamed of it, longed to come here, but something always happened to prevent her. I wonder if she knew the story of the City of Gazelles? Surely, when she rested at night or drowsed round the fire in some desert *ksar*, someone – one of her 'companions of the carpet' – must have propped himself on his elbow and begun: 'One day, a Bedouin of El Oued was lost in the desert. . .'

Ghardaïa: Five towns are scattered over the oasis of the Mzab, but only Ghardaïa possesses an hotel and welcomes visitors. I am here almost by chance, having wanted to go further South – to Tamanrasset perhaps – but finding no means of transport. Another native lorry bumped me over another track where upturned oil-cans mark a route long ago obliterated by sand. I recognize at once that this place is *different*, though I don't yet understand in what way. The Mozabites are unlike the other races in this part of the Maghreb – fair-skinned Berbers, Kabyls, and that rather mysterious Chaamba tribe which speaks its own language. They are stocky, thick-set men, dressed in dull-coloured *gandourahs* and ungenerous turbans. Grocers by tradition, trading in all the cities and villages of Algeria and beyond the frontiers in Tunisia and Morocco. I

Ghardaia

have seen them weighing couscous or sugar in all the places where I have stopped to shop. 'At the Mozabite's,' people say, when one asks where coffee or oil or soap are to be found. They are said to be cunning and acquisitive, ready to wait five, six years without a visit home, while the account swells in the savings-bank. I wonder what it buys? Respect, probably, and a little garden in the palmery, or gold ornaments for a rarely-seen wife, or a dower for daughters?

On the day of my arrival, I thought something unusual must have happened. There was a stirring and muttering in the streets; men walked with downcast eyes or talked in small groups in low voices which seemed to be anxious. I thought I might be mistaken, for it is difficult to detect anything unusual in such a strange and almost eerie place.

I was right. Jean Bertrand, the young French schoolmaster, has told me the story. He has lived here for five years, he speaks the language and is curious about the people. He listens and observes and learns things which the French do not ordinarily bother to know.

I note the story as he told it to me:

Last year, he says, a French boy came out here to teach in

a school like the one in which he himself works, a place where Arab, Mozabite and a few European children get a rudimentary education. He gradually became more and more sad and depressed; he even changed physically, as if he was fading away, but he could not, or perhaps would not give any reason for his sickness, nor would he consent to return home. Finally, he committed suicide and was buried in the Catholic graveyard on the outskirts of Ghardaïa. Some time later, his family applied to have the body returned to France. There were the usual formalities and delays then, exactly on the day of my arrival, the parents, the local grave-digger and a few officials met to open the grave. When the coffin appeared, they realized that someone had been there before them. A ram's skull and a number of magic symbols (even Bertrand, who had the confidence of the Mozabites, has not discovered what they were) had been placed on it and the earth tidily rearranged. The news spread, of course, like wildfire; by midday, the whole oasis knew that someone had been drawing off the magic powers which remain in the corpse of a man who has died by his own hand.

Maybe this story will seem childish, mere superstition, when I get back to Europe. For the moment, I am forced to believe that this event has produced a strange, creepy atmosphere. It weighs on the town like a fog, sharp, sly glances, questioning: 'Is he the thief of the Frenchman's potency?'

This is an all-male town. Once the girls become nubile, they are quickly married off and never appear again, at least until they are really old, when they can occasionally be seen in the marketplace. I have been strolling through streets so narrow that one can hardly walk two abreast, between high, windowless façades which are like fortresses rather than homes. How do those imprisoned women live there while their husbands are away making their fortunes in Algiers or Constantine? Bertrand tells me stories of Europeans who hear soft, whistling calls as they pass through these streets. Some of them, he says, have simply disappeared, never to be seen again, but nothing can be proved.

Ghardaia – the market place

When I walk in the market or open spaces, throngs of little girls come running to flutter around me like butterflies. Their dresses are pink, yellow, orange, purple; their hair is braided with many-coloured ribbons. They seize my hands, cover them with laughing kisses, point to my stomach to ask whether I have any children, point to my wedding-ring to ask where my husband is. They dance round me, laughing, singing little snatches of song, then finger my clothes and reach up to touch my hair. None of them can be more than twelve years old. Perhaps they sing and dance with such exuberant gaiety because they know the prison walls are soon going to close round them for ever.

156

Beni Isguen, the holy city of the Mozabites – a cold, quiet, austere place governed by its *talebs*, who keep a tight hand on their flock and enforce the Mozabite laws. Yesterday, towards the end of the afternoon, I visited the carpet shop, where an impassive dealer sat like a great maggot in his corner, whispering enormous prices. I was handling the lovely, inaccessible carpets when a hoarse, moaning sound broke out from the nearby mosque, joined by another, then another. The *talebs* were blowing their horns to signal sun-down and time for all non-Muslims to leave the city. A young man who had been squatting at the back of the shop leapt up, seized my hand and pulled me to the door. 'Time to go.' Hurrying me through empty streets, where the horn-blasts echoed between high, blank walls, then the city gate and out on to the sandy road leading back to Ghardaïa, the last notes of the horns dying away behind me.

Ghardaia

Back in Algiers, staying in Mademoiselle Robert's little boarding-house. No table, because it had never occurred to her that so strange an activity as writing might take place in her establishment.

I spread my papers out on my bed. Everything has to be sorted out. My book is half-planned in my head. But there has been all the rest – the people and places that had nothing to do with Isabelle. There were times, indeed, when I entirely forgot her and just went where the hasard of a jeep or a lorry led me. Sometimes there came a moment's temptation, never to stop, to go on wandering indefinitely, or perhaps to settle for a few months in one of those white, onion-domed cubes in El Oued.

So all the material directly concerning Isabelle goes into a big manilla envelope. There are visits to old, old men of the Arab Bureau or the *mehari* regiments, caught by retirement, living in neat villas on the outskirts of Biskra or Bou Saâda, trying to grow roses in sandy gardens with the help of amused convict-gardeners supplied by the military tribunals. They have vague memories of Isabelle, think of her chiefly as a trouble-maker, going to places where she had no business to be, interfering in native affairs. Sometimes they remember her and Si Mahmoud as two separate people, or they confuse Si Mahmoud with Sliman the Spahi, whom Isabelle so inexplicably married.

But here in Algiers there has been Capitaine Cauvet, aged ninety. He remembers Isabelle well: 'They told me there was a lady to see me. A young Arab boy came in; I thought it was the lady's servant but it was Miss Eberhardt herself. She dined with me and my officers. I was in charge of the annexe at El Oued then. She talked well, I don't deny that, but we couldn't understand what she was doing there. When she went riding in the desert, staying away for days and nights, we thought she must be spying for Germany, who had its eye on North Africa at that time. Later, I understood her better. She was a sort of poet, I think. She had been initiated into one of the Islamic confraternities, mystics who believed in something

158

they called the Great Unity and wanted to become part of it. I couldn't approve, but I realized there was no harm in her and I defended her as best I could.'

There has been Madame Barrucand too. She has been hoarding Isabelle's letters for half a century. Professor Dhermingem told me: 'She won't let you see them. She flies into a rage if one even mentions them.' But she did let me see them. She scooped them out of a cupboard where they lay pell-mell on the shelves and threw them on the table and hobbled away, leaving me alone in the dim, cat-smelling room

There they were, letters to that half-crazed family in Geneva, to her brother Augustin in Marseilles; to Sliman the Spahi; long missives to Victor Barrucand himself – letters meant for publication in his review.* And the mud-stained manuscripts rescued by General Lyautey's legionaries from the wrecked *gourbi* after the flood at Ain Sefra.

There is nothing now to keep me in Algiers. Madame Rey and the Consul and other French I have met here cannot understand how I managed to travel so far alone. They imagine wild adventures in dangerous places. They warn me not to go alone into the Casbah, because of politics, and the movement for independence, and Arabs being people not to be trusted. Perhaps they are right. Here, I am in a different world, one which is perhaps more complicated and dangerous to explore then were those great white dunes where people are still dreaming of the buried city of El Menzeha.

Next year, the soldiers will be gone and civilian functionaries will be sent out from France. They will have tidy offices, I expect, and keep all the rules laid down in the constitution. I suppose too that they will always wear shoes and reports will be sent back punctually to Paris.

---

* Victor Barrucand was the editor of *Les Nouvelles*, an Algerican daily paper, and the editor of a journal, *Akhbar*. Isabelle Eberhardt was living in a small house that was destroyed by a flood, in which she drowned. General Lyautey was a distinguished French colonial administrator in North Africa.

VIII

Circumstances led me to Malaga and held me there throughout a winter and a spring. I had no idea at the time that I was watching the last, faltering footsteps of Franco's Spain. Nor indeed did any of the Spaniards I met there seem to suspect that anything might succeed Franco but some kind of neo-Franco.

Spain confused me. Its geographical distance from the rest of Europe seemed insufficient to account for the feeling of alienation it engendered. Where was I? Into what alien world had I been projected simply by motoring over the Pyrenees? I sat beneath the flame-tree in our little garden, gazing out across the Mediterranean, which should have been the same as that which bordered the French coast, but was somehow different. A thread of railway-line ran between the garden and the sea. *Atencion al tren* read a notice-board, but wandering goats cropped between the rails and the little train puffed along them only twice a day, once down to Malaga station, and once away from it. *Chilimoya. . . chilimoya. . .* called the fruit-woman at seven each morning, stretching up her basket to our window. Fishermen, rowing across the bay, dipped their oars to a slow rhythm which suggested they were thinking of something else. Omnipresent folklore obscured the landscape, like a fog, sometimes lifting for a few seconds to reveal an estate agency or an electric pylon, then blotting them out again before one could be sure what one had seen.

I searched for clues to this secret country and came on this:

The cleaver, the wagon-wheel, the dagger, the prickly beards of the peasants, the naked moon, the fly, the damp cupboard, the débris, the lace-clothed saints, the whitewash and the sharp line of porches and glazed balconies, everything is covered over, here in Spain, with a fringe of death's

160

grass; everywhere there are signs and allusions, perceptible to the attentive spirit, that prefigure our own selves stiffened in death. . .

Federico García Lorca wrote that and offered it across the years as a sign, or a key. He was murdered near here, somewhere in the beige mountains behind the town and for all those years they had been trying to forget him. But it was no good; he was too much part of Spain, probed her too deeply, and already he was creeping back, like so many Republicans exiled to France or Mexico, and his play *Yerma* was being performed at the Teatre Real in Madrid. 'One can't go on hating for ever,' said Señor Fernandez, my counsellor on the Spanish Mind. His voice betrayed a certain regret for a weakness inherent in mankind. Hatred is a noble sentiment, especially in Spain, and I think he was sorry it could not be eternal.

JOURNAL

The prefiguration of death which Lorca detected in all things Spanish is perhaps the real explanation of Spain. This is a tragic country moulded out of indifference and immobility. Goya and El Greco told the real truth about it and nothing essential has changed since their times. The rest is a show put on by man or nature. Here in Malaga, unlike the austere Northern regions through which we passed on the way, everything favours the show-makers. Elderly English couples sit in front of the cafés on the Avenida, sipping their wine and dissecting their boiled shrimps, sunning away their rheumatism, congratulating each other on the climate. The bougainvillaea and hibiscus trees are in full flower; the sea is a rich, dark blue; a fiesta of some kind has always just been or is just about to be. 'The Spaniards are so *gay*,' explains the General's wife. And so they are. They are as gay as the deformed monstrosities who frolic in the Goya drawings in the Prado, or the men and women who danced themselves to death in thirteenth-century Paris when the plague was at its height. They are dedicated to death, and to Spanish death at that. Here, death and hell are inseparable conceptions. You cannot think of one without being forced to think of the other. In the little rococo parish church, neat and sweet among its roses and geraniums, you find a painted frieze showing an enthroned Christ, borne up on a pillow-cloud, smiling indifferently into space; the lower part of the tableau consists of figures, moulded in wax, writhing among red plastic flames. On weekdays the flames are not specially striking but they are hollow, and on Sundays they are lit up from the inside and one can almost smell the sizzling sinners. The young *novilleros* who came down for the Epiphany bull-fight (the fully-fledged *matadores* are away in South America for the winter season) went to Mass there before their fight. The great black bulls which charged into the arena a few hours later must have a special significance which no non-Spanish fighter could recognize.

The Epiphany *corrida* has been advertized all over the town. Shop windows flower with posters showing an exquisitely handsome matador executing an impeccable veronica as the bull misses him by a hair's-breadth. There is even a poster in the bay window of the Circulo Malagueño. It half-screens the usual view of city notables nodding over their newspapers or sipping jerez. 'It won't be a top-class fight,' says Señor Fernandez. 'But the young matadors come down here to try their hands and show off in case some impresario is looking on. The older men become more cautious.'

So here we are, second row *sol y sombra*. An American *aficionado* tells everyone within earshot just what they may expect, he knows the bull-breeder, trouble once over a sawn-off horn; matrons fan themselves with their programmes; little boys, slippery as fishes, dart through the gates, dive under the nearest seats; attendants rush shouting to root them out, others slip in behind their backs. Twenty minutes after time, a ripple of excitement. The knightly picadores ride in, festooned lances held at the level; then the slim boy in his costume of light, proudly stalking the arena, saluting with his sword the grandee presiding in his box decorated with garlands of paper flowers. The grandee has a big black moustache and a big black hat. He has a stout wife, all in black and three daughters on the

stands facing out into this space of colour & noise,
he stands looking stupid & bewildered, paws the ground & trots forward into the ring. A picador advances at him, jabs with his lance, a thread trickles down the shiny black flanks...

A bullfight should be all beginning & no end. The beginning is the highest of festivals. It recreates ancient Crete. The charging bull is the Minotaur; the toreador is the bull-leaper; the spectacle is ritual & sacrifice. The gods are looking on, applauding a failed pass. Blood & death are in the air. But it doesn't last. We have moved too far away from Crete & Theseus & the Minotaur & from sacrificial rites. The tormented bulls are nearer the truth. There is something of the small slaughter-house. At the end the corpse is dragged by the legs through the sawdust & away to the butchers. Tomorrow, bits of it will hang among other shapeless slabs of meat with a ticket "Toro der ..."

There is even a poster in the Club window, screening our usual view of the city notables reading their newspapers between sips of xxxs.

way to becoming as stout as Mama. They applaud. The youngest girl leans forward on the rail, gazing at the torero with loving, hungry eyes. The arena explodes in a clamour of trumpets as the doors swing open.

The bull-fight, like quite a lot of other things, should be all beginning and no end. The beginning is the highest of festivals. The audience may never have heard of ancient Crete, but for the moment, that is where they are. Blood and death are in the air; they are watching a ritual and a sacrifice. Somewhere in his underground labyrinth, the Minotaur is snorting and pawing the ground. The matador is the bull-leaper. The gods are here, too, looking down from Olympus, ready to applaud a brilliant pirouette or whistle in derision at a failed pass.

It doesn't last. The black bull stands framed in the doorway, gazing out into this space of colour and noise. Surely he ought to stamp and bellow and charge out into the ring? Instead he stands there, looking stupid and bewildered. Grooms prod him forward and at last he paws crossly at the ground and trots forward into the ring. A picador rides at him, jabs with his lance, a scarlet thread trickles down the shining flank. We have moved too far from Crete and Theseus and the Minotaur and sacrificial rites. Goya's tormented bulls are nearer the truth. Nowadays, there is something of the smell of the slaughter-house, in spite of the gallant attitudes and the President's ladies leaning over the barrier, crying Brava! Brava!, nearly swooning with emotion. At the end, the corpse is dragged by one leg through the sawdust, and away to the butcher's. Tomorrow, bits of it will hang among other shapeless slabs of meat with a ticket: *Aqui se vende carne de toro de tidia.*

Early morning is the time for truth. The market is sleepily opening, the town delivered over to donkeys and mules, to a thousand stray dogs on the hunt for scraps. And delivered over, above all, to the sub-world of Andalusia, which is the world of Goya, merely prolonged over another century and a half. Malaga is still peopled by dwarfs, deaf-mutes, creatures swollen into a mass of formless flesh, men with embryo buds in the place of legs and arms. They push and pull each other into place, calculating the length of wall where the winter sun will strike soonest and shine longest and settle along it in rows, glued till nightfall to the grey stone. The blind are being led out by the local agents of the lottery, spaced at regular intervals along the streets, with their handfuls of tickets, all ready for the day's work.

By mid-morning, although this sub-world is more populous than ever, it has become semi-invisible. The show has been set up. Gleaming Mercedes-Benz purr past the convoys of donkeys; the café terraces are crowded with foreigners and elegant Spaniards, holding out their feet to shoe-blacks who look like hungry cats and propose 'señoritas' or contraband watches as they polish. Business is in full though languid swing for those subjected to work; down by the sea-front, magnificently free young men play endless football; Army officers throng the smart bars, sipping Jerez; stout priests pace in twos and threes, occasionally abandoning an unresponsive hand to the lips of female parishioners. 'Why,' I fret to Don Fernandez, 'are there so many lame and blind, so many idiots and men and women born legless and armless? Is it poverty, or syphilis, or some missing chemical?' Don Fernandez stares around him; he is trying hard, but he simply does not see what I see. 'There is a lot of poverty,' he says doubtfully. But the *cour des miracles* does not exist for him.

Like a Victorian father, General Franco shields his people from politics and sex. No one has heard of Brigitte Bardot and at the evening *paseo* the girls pass in groups, wearing neat dresses that gloss over their figures, and drooping Andalusian eyelashes at male greetings. A certain number of French and American films do manage to wriggle through the censorship but the stars have been re-dressed in suitable clothes and thus look curiously unfamiliar on the hoardings. They have become Nice Girls, an example instead of an invitation. As for the real-life nice girls, there is an indigo blush of Moorish blood beneath the smooth olive skin and they have the sort of huge

165

black eyes which suggest their owners might be safer shut away in harems. Instead, they are hurried into female Phalangist organizations. There is one just next door to us – a large, square house from which troops of lovely creatures march out, swinging their arms and singing, to volley-ball or gymnastics at the sports-ground. They are doing the equivalent of military service and will emerge from it, if Franco gets his way with them, clean-limbed and clear-eyed, with *Todo por la Patria* engraved on their hearts. The picture is rather spoilt by the row of young men who squat on their heels along the pavement, gazing up fixedly, hour after hour, at the windows. Sex, like other underground activities, is a matter of patience.

As for politics, they have been smoothed out of daily life. The newspaper we buy at the kiosk has drifted slowly down from Madrid and may be three or four days old. Even the local paper is likely to be a left-over from yesterday or the day before. Nobody seems to mind. There will be nothing in it anyway except the football results, which everyone has heard over the wireless, an article on the saint of the day and a picture of the Minister of this or that at some banquet. Some of the Madrid papers report a good deal of international news but home affairs rarely add up to a single column. 'Nobody cares,' says Don Fernandez. 'Politics for us means ministers becoming very rich up in Madrid. It has always been like that and always will be. If that were to change, Spain would not be Spain any more. We would be homesick, as we would be if we were transplanted to a foreign country.'

He strikes a match, throws it away, strikes another. If the match explodes into a firework, there will be a secret message under the tip and that means a big prize. All over Malaga – and over Spain, Don Fernandez tells me – people strike matches, endlessly. Matches are a State monopoly and this is just one of the lotteries which keep Spain going. Lotteries replace taxation and the more there are, the better people like it. Even the poorest prefer to spend a peseta on the fraction of a ticket rather than on a piece of bread which is swallowed and done with. Hope spurts up with each tiny flame; the pavements are littered with burnt-out matches; and there is always an old, old woman, or a maimed veteran of the civil war pushing yet another box under one's nose, swearing that this one will bring you luck.

So life slips by, painless and sterilized if you are on the right side of the hunger line; and even if you are not there are plenty of free amusements and fiestas and hope to be purchased for the smallest coin in the country. Only thinking is an unhealthy activity, not to be encouraged, but thinking once got the country into real trouble and few people want to do it. A famous doctor told me the other day about the weekly radio programme in which he takes part. There is always a legal expert, a priest, a 'man in the street', who is really a well-known radio speaker, and himself. A question of general interest is chosen each week and discussed in its different aspects. I asked what sort of question, and he told me: 'Last week it was: Should Christmas trees be encouraged in Spain? And before that we discussed our national diet and the use of olive oil in our cooking.'

We were bothing thinking the same thing. He sighed and said: 'Yes, it is difficult to discuss questions of importance. Our talks are recorded in advance and must pass three separate censorships – military, ecclesiastical and political. Nothing much is left after that.' But I felt he was resigned, wouldn't really want things to change.

On New Year's Eve, the whole population of Malaga is out on the streets and most of it concentrated in the Calle Larios and the Square with its illuminated fountain, where the hands of the Cathedral clock are slowly moving towards twelve. Everyone is here – the tourists, the beggars, the shopkeepers, the gypsies from the hills, the soldiers from the barracks, the Greek and American sailors from their ships anchored in the harbour. Pedlars dodge among the crowd selling paper caps, cardboard puppets, sweets, castenets and all sorts of little, bright-coloured toys for the children. The grape-sellers hand out their paper bags of grapes, twelve in each bag, one to be

167

eaten at each stroke of the clock as it marks the passage of the old year to the new. Spontaneously, groups of dancers form, shaking ribbonned tambourines or beating a sort of conical-shaped drum as they weave their complicated steps. A circle forms at once, clapping to the rhythm of the dance or breaking into one of the throaty, monotonous Christmas carols we have been hearing all last week, chanted by bands of children through the warm, dark night. Then the group melts into the throng and another forms in its place, and the same hoarse clamour breaks out above the clatter of other tambourines.

Two fiacres edge their way through the crowd, loaded with giggling, swaying, singing women: one of the local brothels having an evening out, escorted and protected by a single, splendid male, all brilliantined side-whiskers, wide-brimmed hat and pale beige suit nipped into a wasp waist which hardly allows him to breathe. There is no mistaking them. The levelling process has hardly begun in Spain and a tart looks like a tart, not just like any other girl. Out of the fiacre they climb, screaming and giggling – mountains of flesh with sumptuous decolletés filled in with false diamonds and holy medals. One of them begins to dance something between a flamenco and a belly-dance, while her colleagues clap vigorously and scream encouragement. Soon they are surrounded by a dense, clapping crowd and the hoarse Christmas carol takes on a wild flamenco rhythm. The women twirl, snappng their fingers, dripping rouge and mascara, a little drunk perhaps, or perhaps maddened by freedom. They are the centre of everything, the success of the evening, luck-bringers for the New Year.

Now the crowd wavers, opens like the Red Sea before the Children of Israel, presses back, still clapping, to allow the passage of a young man in a primitive invalid chair which he propels by turning the wheels with his hands. He is built like an athlete down to the hips, wide-shouldered and made to be tall. Then, below the hips, there is one tiny leg, like that of a five-year old child, protruding bizarrely sideways and out-wards. The other leg is not there at all. The crowd closes up behind him and he stays there in the front row, close to the dancers, laughing and showing his big, white teeth, clapping his hands and shouting jokes. He seems perfectly happy and so does everyone else.

Señora Ortiz, our landlady, invites us to meet her friends at after-dinner coffee. We sit round the warming-table, our knees under its flounced petticoat, the soles of our feet turned up to the *brasero* hidden in its depths. Cold has descended suddenly on Malaga, reminding us that it is winter everywhere else. Tiled floors have become icy to the feet and a chill wind creeps under the doors and through the window-frames. Now and then Señora Ortiz bends, panting, for the flat iron spoon and stirs the charcoal dust. 'Like making an omelette,' she says, 'you lift the edges and stroke inward.' On the wall, there is a semi-life-size portrait of Alfonso XIII, robed, with all his decorations. Señora Ortiz is a monarchist and is always hoping for a return of the Royal Family. At the moment, her main preoccupation is the question of precedence at the wedding of Doña Fabiola Mora y Aragon to King Baudouin of the Belgians. Her finger stabs triumphantly at a copy of *Sur*:

'Listen to this. . . "Representing Spain at the royal wedding will be the Count of Barcelona", then come the Marques of this and that, and at the very bottom of the list, the Marques and Marquesa de Villa Verde.' The pearls heave on her black satin bosom; appreciative chuckles from the Bank Manager and the president of the select Malaga Club. 'How can it have slipped past the censorship? Someone must have got into trouble!' 'But they put it right the next day,' says the Bank Manager. 'The whole paragraph was reprinted, with Franco's son-in-law first and our Infante last.'

They dream for a moment over this mirage of restored tradition produced by a printer's error. They dream of a restoration of the Monarchy. Once a week, they meet in Señora Ortiz' flat to dream aloud, and all over Spain, says Señor Fernandez, other little monarchist circles are meeting, so they believe, in secret. 'Drawing-room monarchists', Señor Fernandez calls them. Not to be taken seriously, but sometimes there are

Communists disguised as Monarchists. They hope for a King like young Juan Carlos, who might introduce a liberal regime. That would bring a revolt by the Army, backed by the Church, and then it would be the turn of a Communist counter-revolution.

That is the nightmare that obsesses the Spanish bourgeoisie. Somewhere, just around the corner, Communists are plotting, concealed in whatever organism happens to be one's personal *bête noire*, and any change, even for the better, will give them their chance. It is this spectre, this shadow army which may or may not be a reality, which maintains Spain in her frozen rigidity of resignation and pessimism – like a man seized with vertigo on a narrow pass, who dares not move backwards or forwards for fear of the abyss beneath his feet.

Nothing of this is said, of course, in our presence. Ladies are there, anyway: the Bank Manager's wife, fatter even than Señora Ortiz, folds of chin encircled with pearls and gold chains, merging into a vast, corseted bosom; Señora Rubroso, the notary's wife, youngish, dressed up to the nines, a gown copied from one of the Paris fashion-magazines, with a skirt barely covering her knees. Both sit silent, only occasionally exchanging a few words with each other. Señor Rubroso speaks French, talking to me as he would talk to a child, asking if I enjoy Spanish cooking, if I have seen the Spanish star who sings so prettily in her new film. He is probably wondering if I am a Communist, as foreigners are so apt to be.

The Calderons run a big *estancia* a few miles from the town, where they grow sugar cane and olives and a few cereals which they coax with infinite difficulty out of the dry soil. They are wealthy people, the most progressive farmers in the region, but their implements are extraordinarily primitive and they still plough with a wooden-bladed plough drawn by oxen. They do very well all the same, because their land is near the sugar factory. When the canes are cut in May and June, they have only to pile them on the big mule-wagons and send them off to be pressed, squeezed and refined without any of the transport expenses that ruin so many farmers.

Conchita Calderon is one of the few people here who have travelled abroad in spite of the low exchange rate and the complicated business of obtaining a passport. A few months in England have upset some of her ideas and given her the uncomfortable feeling that she is living in a sort of no-man's-land, neither Europe nor Africa, which does not quite belong to the past or the present. She welcomes timid reforms which anger or frighten so many of her neighbours. Most people here avoid these by employing workers only by the day or the week and dismissing them when the olive crop has been gathered or the cows have finished calving.

Old Pepe, the Calderon's cowherd, has been taken away for a hernia operation. He lies in a ward in the new, ultra-modern Carlos Haya Hospital for Salaried Workers, looking absolutely lost, his sad, monkey eyes staring unblinkingly above the starchy white sheet. The Director fought with the Germans during the war, in the volunteer Spanish Brigade on the Russian front. His hospital is run with Teutonic efficiency and seems to belong to a different land and a different century. He is immensely proud of his six operating theatres, his iron lung, the fifteen doctors attached to the establishment and the two hundred beds in which the sick, looking utterly terrified, are tended by efficient little nurses. Everything is clean and shining; the place is a huge, stream-lined symbol of Progress.

'You see,' says Conchita, 'you are wrong. Things are moving even here in Andalusia, where the sun makes us lazy and disinclined for change.'

But the hospital is half empty, because there is not much regular employment in this region. This is no place for pay-sheets and forms to be filled with figures. The few salaried workers live in the modern suburbs, encapsulated in new blocks of flats – somewhat jerry-built, but with bathrooms and all amenities. Farm labourers are up before dawn each morning, trudging in twos and threes along the road or the track or over the hills to their *estancia*. City workers set off a little later in buses which unload them in the square by the

171

main Post Office. They are employees of the Municipality, or shop assistants. They wear dark suits of shiny serge, the whitest of white shirts and sober ties. Their names are entered in ledgers, in alphabetical order; they hold cards which ensure them against illness and accident, though they have always been told that such mishaps are due to the will of God; the names of their children are inscribed beneath their own and are worth a few extra pesetas. Whatever they earn is written down, plain for everyone to see, and on Friday evening there will be an envelope with bank notes for the proper amount.

These bus-riders from the suburbs are part of the early-morning truth about Malaga. Yawning in the pale light of Post Office Square, they reveal themselves at once as foreigners, as the outcasts of the city. The real citizens of Malaga are the fisher-people in the slums behind the port – out of work for most of the year because their boats are too fragile to put out into the Atlantic fishing-grounds – and the casual labourers hanging round the docks, and the shoe-blacks and the pedlars and the vast, semi-invisible population that scrapes a living as best it can in any way occasion offers. Señora Ortiz and her friends belong here too, so do the members of the Men's Club, so does the Marques Torrebianco, who presides at the bull-ring. Only the salaried workers with their obligatory insurance and family allowances and sometimes even an old-age pension, are out of place, for the time being, that is. Some day, perhaps not very far into the future, it is they who will become the true citizens of Malaga.

All through the Christmas season and the month of January, the Christmas tombola has drawn crowds to the Larios Square. From ten in the morning till after midnight there is a dense throng round the stalls where a young priest, assisted by some girls from the convent, doles out little envelopes at a few centavos a piece. If you are lucky, it may hold a number which gives you a right to a bar of chocolate or a sham crystal ashtray, or even a radio or a set of graduated saucepans. The tombola is run by *Caridad*, and the proceeds go to build working-class houses – not for those few salaried workers this time, but for anyone whose home is postively crumbling about his ears.

The clergy is taboo in Spain. Not a breath of open criticism may touch them, although their tendency to acquire land, shops and houses rather than attend to the spiritual needs of their parishioners, is a favourite subject of gossip. They regard their colleagues in France with deep suspicion and a few months ago their archbishop issued a letter warning their clergy against 'subversive ideas from across the mountains'. The archbishop of Malaga, however, is rather an exception and is considered to be unusually socially-conscious. For this reason *Caridad* is especially active here, and many of the younger priests act as social workers, doling out medicines, distributing rations to the needy and bullying their wealthy parishioners into taking some kind of interest in the poor. 'The Church has remained indifferent too long,' Father S. explains to me. He is young, pink and plump and has studied in a seminary in New York, from which he has returned with an American accent and a habit of chewing gum. 'We are trying to create a social conscience,' he says. 'It is not enough to give money, the rich must mix with the poor and get to know them.' He holds meetings in his parish and tries to instil languid Andalusian businessmen with his own enthusiasm. 'I have explained to them that if they do not do their part they will go to hell,' he tells me eagerly. 'Once they understand that, they begin to give me money and now they are becoming interested and we are beginning to get results.'

But nobody is in a hurry, everything can wait. Nothing which is, can possibly be as bad as what might be. A new generation has grown up since the Civil War, but it has been reared on stories of its horrors; fathers and uncles were massacred, and the tracts of ruins near the port show where the bombs fell, from whose planes no one quite knows. The feeling of death that Lorca detected in all things Spanish weighs more heavily than ever on this land which should be happy in its sunny beauty, but is sad and still, as if death is the only security for which it can hope.

173

XI

Morocco will be my last journey. I mean, it will be the last time I shall travel in the old way. My life is changing, and so is the world. It will soon be impossible to wander almost by chance, to explore countries hesitating between past and future. It would no longer be safe, it seems, to stroll by moonlight among the white dunes of El Oued and listen for the music of the djinnoun rising out of the hollows. At Ein Gev, they say, there are concrete buildings along the lake-shore, and machine-milkers for the cows, and proper working hours for everyone. London has demolished its ruins, and raised pure, plain office blocks, and created the Welfare State. As for Marseilles, where we are waiting for our trans-Mediterranean passage, the Germans have dynamited the Old Port and the surrounding quarter. Concrete blocks use up the streets where red lamps used to hang above the doorways and women snatched the hats of passers-by and ran giggling into the passages. Down by the port, electric cranes hover over the ships and electric trolleys clang, carrying freight to new, distant docks.

I have always thought of Morocco as a country lying just across the sea, a place of sun and orange-groves, where one went for profit or pleasure. Now it has become another half-way land, ruled by a King who can, or cannot, be counted on. Frightened, bewildered settlers are selling up as best they can, returning to France, or waiting nervously to see what is going to happen. Some day, it will reorganize itself in some way or another. Meanwhile, it is still a shifting land, with the old ways disappearing and new ones not yet established. A place to be explored while it is still time, before it settles down to the routine of an independent state.

I noted everything, pell-mell – places, people and thought,

ready for pruning down to the taste of some review. I wrote in an inconvenient notebook, far too big for travel, but beloved because it was a real book, with a hard cover and blank pages, a publisher's dummy, I suppose. It looks English. Someone must have given it to me back in London. It starts with Morocco, but it must have been in my possession much earlier. The first pages are full of my journey, but afterwards, it has been left blank, probably because I had entered a different phase of my life.

JOURNAL

The white uniformity of Rabat, with its banks and Chamber of Commerce, its cinemas and one-price stores. Close by, there is the Sultan's palace, where unnaturally tall Negroes of the Black Guard stand sentinel beneath ancient arches of pink stone. Sometimes, one can see the Sultan himself, hustling into a Daimler, off to inspect this or that. Sometimes he wears a wreathed turban, sometimes rather sporty European clothes. He looks energetic – youngish, with a touch of ruthlessness and a touch of gentleness. His years of exile have given him an aura of martyrdom which is probably useful when dealing with tribesmen who love symbols and panache. The souks are plastered with lithographs showing a heavy-weight angel grasping him by the hand and dragging him upwards to some idyllic future; his portrait presides over every office and every home and turns up in all sorts of unlikely places – inset in clocks, painted on conch-shells, woven into curtain materials. He is an angel or a demon, depending upon who is speaking to you, but he is always the centre around which the future of the country revolves.

The presence of the French Army is puzzling. What are they doing here? No one seems to know, but young Curton (military service at the air-base) speaks fiercely of protecting French citizens and ensuring *la presence française*, while Moroccans say vaguely: 'On tolerance.' In the evening, the town is full of very young uniformed men, strolling in groups, whistling

175

at girls, nibbling chocolate and gazing at the stills outside the cinema where the credit-titles are written in Arabic. Sometimes they come face to face with a group of green-bereted soldiers from the Royal Army, then their faces grow stiff and cold, and the faces of the darker-skinned men assume exactly the same expression. The two groups freeze into silence and the high French chatter and the throaty Arab talk break out again only when a few yards of neutral ground lies between them.

The Medina is out of bounds to young Curton, so we take him to dinner in the only Arab restaurant in the new town. We eat *tardjine* and *couscous* and *pasteria*. Three months out here have turned all young Curton's ideas upside-down. The high ideals have gone, replaced by that sullen, unreasoning hatred of the Others, which always seems to be waiting deep in our subconscious, ready for a chance to well up and take over. Three months ago, he was full of enthusiasm, he was going to 'find a common ground for Christians and Muslims', he was going to learn Arabic. Now he is angry and frightened. He uses the belittling names which are small defences against primitive terrors. Weighing on the other side of the balance, there are photographs of the mutilated bodies of Europeans murdered in the Meknes riots last October. These photographs are distributed to recruits as soon as they land and several complete strangers have pressed them on me.

They tell me here: Don't go into the Medina. I go, of course, and wander among the indifferent crowds, among flies and the peculiar, universal smell of Arab streets: stale mutton-fat, urine and a mouldy, spicy smell I have not yet identified. No one pays the least attention to me. I might just as well be invisible. No way of telling whether this is due to hostility or just plain lack of interest.

The *bidonville* is another matter. It lies along the sea-front for about two miles and looks rather like an abandoned chicken-farm, dissected by alleys of stamped mud which divide the *douars* of the different tribes. Some of the houses are made like card-castles, with five sheets of rusty corrugated iron stacked up as four walls and a roof, with a crack at one corner for creeping in and out. Others are conical cabins of roughly-bound wicker stakes. Nobody knows how many thousands of Arabs live here, in this place which simply absorbs families and *douars* and even whole tribes, moved up from the hungry South in the hope of finding work in town. Sometimes they surge out into the streets of Rabat in menacing hunger-marches and are driven back by the Royal Army to starve in their proper place.

I have not dared to penetrate far into this vaguely menacing place. I have only been at its edge, near enough to catch the reek of excrement and rotting vegetables, and the peculiar silence of alleys where a few children scratch in the mud, each surrounded by an attendant cloud of flies. Surely poverty in the West is never quite as sordid as urban poverty in Islam? Perhaps Islam is still maladjusted to town life? The primitive nobility of the desert Muslims seems to collapse when it comes into contact with an industrial civilization. Here, I meet town-Arabs, question them, try to grope my way into their minds and I begin to suspect that time and space no longer have quite the same meaning they had to the men who told me their long, rambling stories in the Souf.

Aghouatime

A stork sits all day on her nest built on the low, pink-washed balustrade of my terrace. She stays perfectly still, one leg tucked under her breast, gazing across the carpet of purple bougainvillaea that spreads over the veranda roof, out to the orange-trees and away to the line of cypress-trees which bounds the olive-groves. She pay no attention to the restless movements of the baby storks, but towards evening her mate joins her and the quick, dry clacking of beaks as they exchange the day's news drowns all other sounds. These sounds, which waft across the terrace and through my window are: the cluck-ing of guinea-fowl, cooing of doves, crickets chirping in the rose-beds below, occasional roars from the black bulls tethered in the farm-yard, the soft talk of Arab workmen walking in the paths, the cries of mating frogs in the irrigation channels.

177

Early in the morning, before the heat grows too strong, we explore the estate. Two thousand acres – olives, oranges, apricots, wheat, several hundred head of cattle and two fine flocks of sheep, the little red *douars* of the tenant farmers, surrounded by thick thorn-hedges, with a cow or camel cropping at the scrub by the gate; old people and children indolently scratching at patches of melons and onions; irrigation channels intersecting the plantations, workmen banking them up with clay, and the rich smell of the flooded earth gulping the cold snow-water flowing from the government-owned reservoir in the Atlas mountains.

The men are scything the lucerne field, their white robes swinging with the movement of their scythes, the women following to gather the sheaves, skirts tucked high over their bright silk pantaloons. Beyond the house, they are gathering in the apricot crop, packing the hard yellow fruit – not too ripe, because it will be made into jam in Marrakesh – in wooden crates. A tall black foreman with a whisp of turban wound round his shaven head, strides among the workers, examining the fruit with sharp, black eyes under long, curled lashes. The orange-groves are still thick with fruit and the sun bounces off the shiny rinds like fire on copper. Close behind the groves, the mountains rise up stiff and sharp, with a little cap of snow on the highest peaks.

Our friend Pierre is the owner of all this land. It has taken him thirty years to plough and sow it, force it to bear corn and fruit and pasture for his herds. He leads us out beyond the wheat-fields to the edge of the plantation, where fertile ground gives way to arid red earth, so thick with boulders that only a few patches of scrub and coarse grass can push their way between them. He kicks angrily at a stone in his path; he is always angry now: 'In three years,' he says, 'the whole estate will look like this, just as it did when I bought the land.' He has accepted an Arab offer for less than a quarter of its value and now he hates his wheat and apples and apricots, and his sheep and cows too. He hates his land because of the fate he imagines for it and because he will not be here to see next year's harvesting and lambing. He wants to be done with the place, to get away, back to France, to a safe little house in the suburbs of Paris, or perhaps of Marseilles where the climate will be kinder.

Pierre and his wife Edith are afraid. They have read about the massacres in Meknès and Oued Zem, about the four pro-French *caïds* burned to death in the main square of Marrakesh, just ten kilometres away from here. They know their water-supply can be cut off at any moment. They have received threatening letters from a dismissed cook. Down in the South, just over the Atlas, there is famine and unemployment and the French are the natural scapegoats. One day, perhaps, their sullen workers will set fire to the house and drive the two of them back into the flames when they try to escape, as they did to the Europeans in the Meknes brickworks.

Yet I don't think Pierre has decided to sell out and leave just because he is afraid. There are other reasons, perhaps not entirely clear even to himself. For thirty years he has been absolute master on his own land. When he spoke, his orders were obeyed. *Caïds* in the outlying villages invited him to their *mechouis* rather as children invite their parents to a dolls' tea-party. When the Arabs on his estate were old or ill he was kind to them and they thanked him with long, ritual blessings. There was a place for everyone, and everyone had his place, as if it had been so from the beginning and would remain so for ever. And now, here he is, wandering through his own orchards and the pickers stare as he passes and do not even greet him. He is no longer responsible for them. They belong to unions, which have their representatives on the estate. A Minister in far-off Rabat fixes their wages and decides how much free milk and wheat they must receive. Pierre has been accustomed to shout his orders, to curse when he feels like it. Now he must speak in a new tone of voice. 'Imbecile!' Edith begins to scream at the slow-witted house-boy, but she stifles the word before it is quite uttered: 'The roast is getting cold, Muhammad. Please bring it in.' Neither of them can under-stand who are these hostile people, this new race of men by

Moroccans demonstrating against the French in Meknes

whom they are surrounded. They are lost in a crazy, through-the-looking-glass world from which all the old values have disappeared. Now they grope their way, angry and frightened, and long for, yet dread, escape.

When I set off to visit the new head-caïd, Pierre advises me:

'Call him "Excellency". They all expect it.' But Si Ahmed looks surprised and says: 'But I am not an Excellency.' He is a large, plump young man of twenty-five, naturally jolly, I imagine, but weighed down just now by worries and responsibilities. He was once a secretary in the French administration, without hope of promotion, so he resigned and became a teacher. 'Now I have the chance to work at building a new Morocco,' he says. He builds it by dashing from village to village in his appointed district, scolding the inhabitants about their sanitation, forbidding them to build slaughter-houses on the edge of streams which supply their drinking-water, persuading them to attend classes in the techniques of municipal life. He has to choose *caïds* from villages where no one can read or write and try to find incorruptible men where corruption has always been the rule. Then there is the office again, and patient queues squatting along the corridors, waiting to expound long-winded grievances arising from inextricable muddles. Si Ahmed listens and tries to explain new methods, and when he has finished, the men bless him and begin all over again, chanting through the same story.

Si Ahmed knows that his country still needs the French and cannot yet get on without them but he must not say so in public. There are times when the truth must not be told, times for silence and pretences. Morocco is teaching me that truth can be dangerous, and should be treated warily, like other dangerous things – bombs, for instance.

Marrakesh

Before Independence, the Place Djmaa-el-Fna was given over to snake-charmers, Chleu dancers, players of lute and *rhebaya*, tellers of stories and itinerant dentists. The new régime disliked such old-fashioned activities. They were promptly banished and Djmaa-el-Fna became a car park. But the old habitués were merely waiting for the first fine flush of modernity to pass. Now they are drifting back and the rare cars huddle round the edge of the square among rows of stalls selling cheap brooches, roasted peanuts, bright pink sweets melting in the sun and art-silk table-mats stamped with the Sultan's head. Only in the centre of the square the dancers lope through their complicated and sinuous game of follow-my-leader; a skeleton man bangs on a tambourine, calling up his audience to hear some legendary story from the Atlas mountains; old women crouch over their little piles of pebbles and bottles, ready to charm husbands into being more faithful or more ardent, or whatever they want them to be. 'They will bring in the tourists,' says the Governor's wife briskly.

The Governor lives in the finest house in what was still the European Quarter a year ago. It has arches and balconies; it is surrounded by roses as big as cabbages and guarded by sleepy soldiers. His wife is one of those formidable, immensely active New Women the Arab States have been throwing up during the last decade. She has a relentlessly purposeful jaw and subtle eyes, always looking for weakness or credulity in the adversary. We drink mint tea and eat *cornes de gazelle* while three doe-eyed girls squat on the floor and gaze at her with adoration. 'You must not listen to the settlers' stories,' she says. 'Our whole nation is united behind the Sultan now.' 'What about the Southern territories?' I ask. 'And the Army of Liberation that passes arms to the Algerians, who are your enemies, and fight beside them on occasion?' She stares at me, cool and ironical: 'We are on the side of our Muslim brothers in Algeria. How could it be otherwise?' Then she tells me how hard it is to administer a State where the French kept everything for themselves, all its functionaries imported from France and never a job for a Moroccan. When she talks of the French, her big brown eyes narrow and her lips tighten: 'They came out here, people who were nothing in their own country and behaved as if they were princes and despised our people.' I say: 'It was the same in India,' but this is a *faux pas*. 'That was quite different,' she retorts. 'Indians are coloured people.'

Tisnit
South of Mogador [now Essaouira], the signs of famine begin. Bare branches of trees stripped by locusts two years running;

two-dimensional sheep and donkeys licking at empty tins among the stones, tottering and dying bleakly on their backs. The only vegetation – forests of arganier trees with their bitter fruit, where black goats perch like birds in the branches, gnawing at the bark, crunching it to keep themselves alive. Then Agadir with its abandoned factories and fine avenues ending in scrubland, gradually rotting away among its planned and unachieved grandeur. Because of the fear of the Army of Liberation, there are houses with fine orange-groves for sale in the region for the price of two years' harvest.

After Agadir, the country changes to the blood-red, stony *reg*, dotted with poisonous cactus. How far can we go in safety? No one can say, or rather, everyone has a different story. Danger is always just out of sight, or a hundred kilometres away, or lurking in an apparently abandoned *douar* perched on a rocky prominence. The rebel army is somewhere in the South. Nobody knows just where, and I begin to suspect that nobody really cares. Perhaps all this is just a blown-up village feud, big *caïds* with interests of their own, urging rival cousins to kill and grab.

Suddenly, the road is barred with barbed-wire. A sergeant scrutinizes our papers, turning them doubtfully this way and that. An officer is called up. A long slow discussion. The officer gestures towards red, forbidden land: 'Bad men. . . You not go. . .' But other soldiers, wearing a different uniform stoll up, stand chatting with his men, watching us with sideways glances which are neither hostile nor friendly, but merely curious.

The gates are low arches pierced in the city's double ramparts. Between the walls there is a sort of lane where the sand is coarse and evil-smelling because the sun never reaches it and it is used as a lavatory. The second archway opens on to a muddle of arcades and criss-crossing of narrow lanes, and tiny shops where the merchants sleep all day long among their heavy silver ornaments, bright rugs, leather sandals, and engraved copperware which they will never sell because there are no more tourists to buy them. Now there are just Negroes and Berbers and blue-veiled Touaregs come from the great distances which mean nothing to them, standing beside their camels, selling their firewood with disdainful patience. At the deserted bus-station an arrow points to *Dakar, 2,300 km*, and another promises vaguely, *All directions*. But the East and South gates are barricaded and manned by armed sentinels. This is the last outpost of the Sultan's power and all the territory beyond is controlled by the Army of Liberation. Sometimes the sound of distant gunfire suggests that a battle is in progress, but soldiers of both armies come freely into town to buy provisions. They hand in their weapons to the sentinels at the gate, then stroll under the arcades, bargain in the market, greet relatives or sit gossipping in the shadow of the walls until they are rounded up by their officers.

Since we can go no further, we have taken a room in the one hotel. It is about to close down, its hall encumbered with trunks and packing-cases. 'Who would stay to be a servant where he has once been master?' asks the Corsican landlord, banging his chairs into a pyramid on the dining-room floor. A corner of the room remains in service, just for ourselves, and each evening Monsieur Santini tosses us up an omelette from eggs which get staler each day.

I go every morning to the *Caïd*'s palace, but always the guards make signs to tell me he is not at home. I realize now that he never will be at home for me because he guesses I want him to give me a pass for the South.

Each day we say we will leave tomorrow, yet we stay on. We wait for nothing special and for no good reason; we have simply succumbed to the barbarous lethargy of this country. One day, soon no doubt, we shall make up our minds to head back for Casablanca, and meanwhile, we are still here.

Yet Monsieur Santini is only waiting to be rid of us, and foreigners are unwelcome in the town. Nothing is said, there is never an angry or even hostile word. I have merely become invisible. I feel the light touch of the men's robes as they brush past me in the street, but they never allow their eyes to rest on me. When I buy bread or dates in the market, there is just the murmur of a price, but never a greeting. When I tried to bargain for a bracelet in the silver souk, the merchant pulled a fold of his cloak across his face and muttered that it was not for sale.

I feel insubstantial, I have become a wandering ghost, yet this very apartness renders me more sensitive to the resonances of small events I observe in the town.

A public writer sits cross-legged at a street corner, impassively taking dictation from a soldier. The soldier gesticulates, clenches his fists, rolls his eyes, searches desperately for inspiration. Nothing comes. A formula is suggested, rejected. Another suggestion, rejected again, accepted at last in a mimic of despair at its inadequacy. Something like: 'Trusting this finds you well as it leaves me at present'? A woman in some distant village will take the message to another scribe and ask: 'Tell me what he says to me?', and weep when she hears it so brief and cold.

Five blind beggars stand in a row, seeming never to sleep or eat, chanting an unending prayer to Sidi Lachmi. The words are repeated over and over again and presently I detect in them an unformulated message. Time, it suggests, can have many different meanings and sometimes it can mean nothing at all. When there is no light or darkness, the rhythm of days and night is perhaps less significant than the grunt of thanks which interrupts the chant when a coin has been placed in an outstretched palm.

Two soldiers play dice behind the mosque. One wears the green beret of the Sultan's Army; the other, the khaki turban of the Army of Liberation. Perhaps they are brothers, living one on each side of an unmarked frontier. A dice flicks into the air; a finger jabs a dot into the sand; one of them has won, the other lost. They rise, link little fingers and stroll away in the direction of the gate. There, I suppose, they will recover their rifles and rejoin their regiments and use words like 'rebel' and 'traitor'.

The story-teller sits, sunk on his haunches, hands tucked into sleeves, the folds of his grey and brown-striped *gandourah* spreading around him: a great spider crouched on the rough earth, at the centre of his web. The circle of listeners listens with such intensity that no one notices me as I sink to the ground at its edge.

The man's face is dark, like the colour of dark earth, swathed in greyish muslin, seamed with deep, parallel furrows, eyes set in wrinkles of dark flesh, one of them covered with a blue-white film of glaucoma. The lips hardly move and the sound issues from them in a continuous, unaccented, unpausing flow which seems to rise from a source deep in the throat.

A small boy, earth-coloured like his father or grandfather (impossible to tell the man's age), sits behind the story-teller, holding on his lap an instrument like a small, two-stringed banjo. Now and again he twangs a chord, interrupting this flow of sound in which I can detect neither words nor phrases. Then a murmur, apparently of approval or agreement, rises from the circle of listeners.

I sit here apart, unnoticed, among these alien and possibly hostile men, listening with them to the same hypnotic confusion of sounds. Gradually, these sounds begin to take shape and it seems to me that they carry the same essential message to them and to me. The story-teller is telling a story which I cannot understand, but behind and beyond that story he is saying that certain things have always been and always will be. He is saying that we are all carried along by the same eternal rhythm which we perceive through whatever words or music happen to be familiar to us. Here I am, seated in the scuffed sand among these dark-skined, turbanned men, but I might just as well be back in the Eisteddfod tent in Rhos, watching through the open entrance the faint, blue mountains fade into the clouds hanging above Snowdon. The little, dark man from Pennal is up there on the platform, reciting a very long *cynghadedd* popem. At first he gesticulates, declaims, then he grows quiet and stands there, small and immobile, while the incomprehensible words flow from his lips. He is telling me the sme untellable things as the Moroccan story-teller. Just now, for instance, the story-teller is telling of a moment when I saw the twin towers of Chartres rising up behind a yellow plain, outlined against a dark blue sky. The towers are still there, exactly as they were then. It will be enough to drive some day at the right season through the ripe cornfields of the Beauce, until they come into sight. But I shall never see them again at the exact moment when a small, dark aeroplane swooped across their silhouette to loose its bomb. Pure beauty and pure terror, mingling in a world beyond words.

Now the rhythmic flow falters and stops. A rustle and stir among the seated men; the story-teller has become aware of my presence; perhaps someone there in the listening circle has made a sign to him. Silence now, a slow turning of heads, watchful, hooded eyes. Behind the eyes, there are thoughts: I am an intruder, no business to be here, a foreigner, a spy, a bringer of bad luck. No way to explain to the story-teller that he was speaking to me too. He knows only his own way of telling and speaking. One day, perhaps, some *caïd* or desert captain will decree that he may not use his own words or tell his own story. Maybe, someone will do the same to me, and to the Bard from Pennal, and to a lot of other people who listen and try to put what they hear into words. Maybe, that won't matter after all. The river will go on flowing and no one, ever, will be able to dam its course.

I rise and turn away from the watching men and walk quietly back to the hotel. It is time to be going, anyway. Monsieur Santini's crates are being loaded on to a lorry at the door; our supper-table in the corner of the dining-room has not been set. We shall fetch the car from the yard and drive off over the bumps and pitholes of the neglected road to Agadir. Then there will be Mogador, then Casablanca, and at Casablanca it will be easy to get a passage to Marseilles.

Acknowledgements

For permission to reproduce illustrations, the author and publishers are grateful.

pp. 7, 8: Peter Owen Ltd and the Estate of Anaïs Nin, from *The Journals of Anaïs Nin 1934–1939*, edited by Gunther Stohlmann (1967,) p. 13: The Trustees of Imperial War Museum; p. 48: Editeurs français réunis, from *On m'appelait la comtesse rouge* by Catherine Karolyi (1969); p. 66: courtesy of the Gimpel family; p. 115: by J. Feuille © C.N.M.H.S./S.P.A.D.E.M.; pp. 149, 154, 156, 157: courtesy of the office Algérien d'Action Economique et Touristique; p. 180: Associated Press.

They also acknowledge the assistance of the Jewish Programmes Material Project.

188